IMAGES
of America

MISSIONS OF
CENTRAL CALIFORNIA

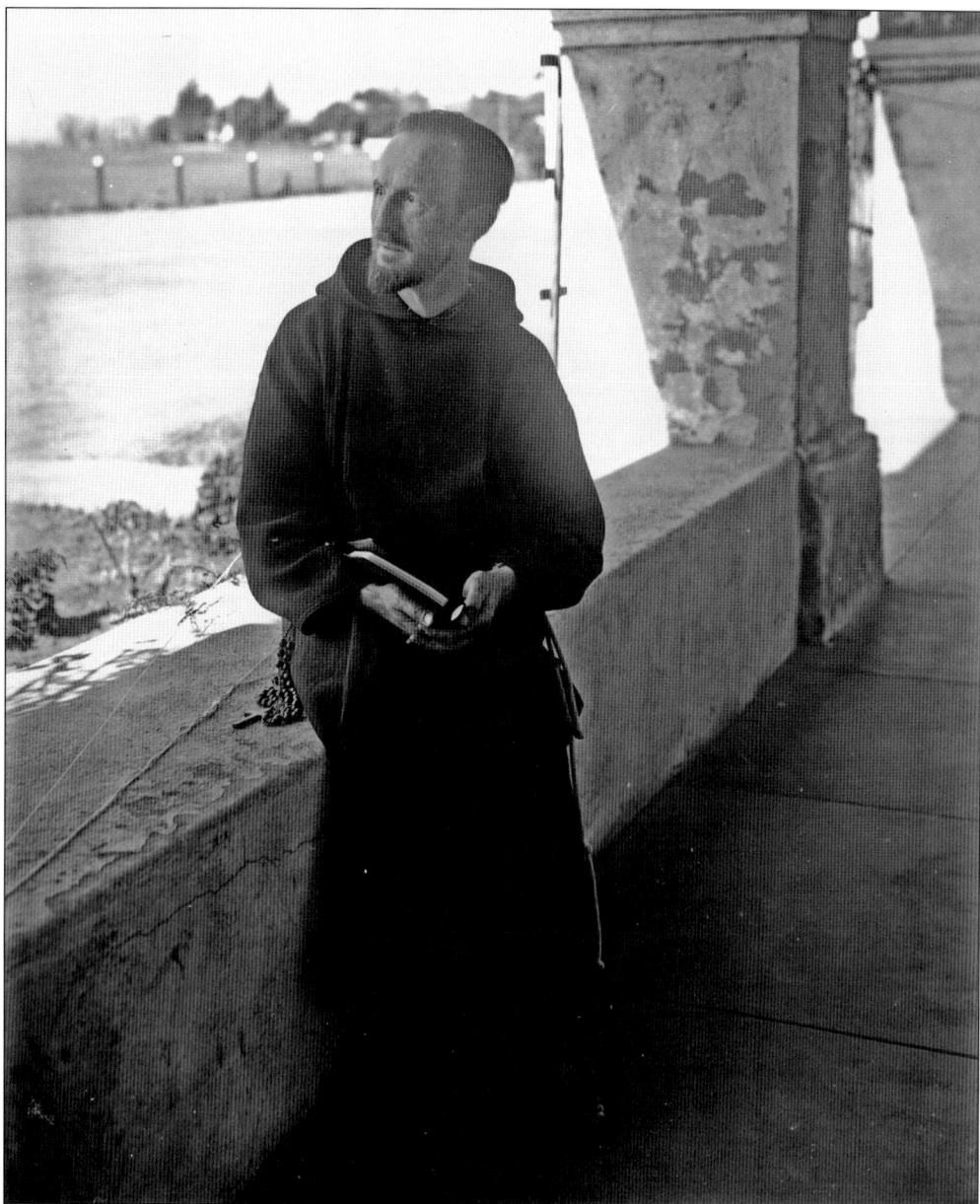

Surrounded by Mission Santa Inés's serene grounds yet living in a modern world, Fr. Vincent Kerwick shows a pensive mood around 1928 at the center of California's earliest history in present-day Solvang. This 19th mission had been established in 1804 in the beautiful Santa Ynez River Valley, 45 miles northeast of Santa Barbara. (Anderson Family Collection.)

On the Cover: Old Mission Santa Inés, Virgen y Mártir, is pictured around 1937 with its pastor, Father Kerwick. The mission, under the Capuchin Franciscan fathers' management since 1924, has been completely restored and rebuilt along with most of the *convento* wing. The existing church was built in 1817 by Fr. Estévan Tápis, mission president of California's Spanish missions. Considered one of the best examples of native Indian artistry, the mission still serves local Chumash and the neighboring community of Solvang. (Anderson Family Collection.)

IMAGES
of America

MISSIONS OF
CENTRAL CALIFORNIA

Robert A. Bellezza

ARCADIA
PUBLISHING

Published by Arcadia Publishing
Charleston, South Carolina

Printed in the United States of America

Library of Congress Control Number: 2012952042

For all general information, please contact Arcadia Publishing:
Telephone 843-853-2070
Fax 843-853-0044
E-mail sales@arcadiapublishing.com
For customer service and orders:
Toll-Free 1-888-313-2665

Visit us on the Internet at www.arcadiapublishing.com

Warm wishes to my brother Don, Elisabeth, and the family back on the east coast. I owe a valuable part of my early curiosity of history to those placid shores.

In 1603, upon landing along these shores during his historic voyage, Sebastián Vizcaíno named the harbor and waterway straights of the Channel Islands after legendary martyr Saint Barbara. In the legend, she was slain by her father, who then perished from a sudden lightning bolt. Revered over the centuries, Saint Barbara lives today as a symbolic icon of the Mission Santa Bárbara and the surrounding community. (Author's collection.)

CONTENTS

ACKNOWLEDGMENTS

The Library of Congress Prints & Photographs Online Collection has supplied the majority of images within this volume and makes possible a review of California's founding architectural landmarks practically lost through centuries of age, deterioration, and neglect. California's mission buildings were rescued only after the majority had suffered irreversible weathering and ruin to the adobe walls. The Historic American Building Survey, employing the Civilian Conservation Corps (CCC) and photographers from the 1933 New Deal, documented the decay of the many iconic structures. Unless otherwise indicated, all images are courtesy of the Library of Congress, Historic American Buildings Survey/Historic American Engineering Record/Historic American Landscapes Survey.

By the beginning of the 20th century, efforts had been made to preserve the earliest missions, often built and decorated entirely by California natives. Several photographs within this volume are released for the first time from the author's collection and from the Anderson family's collection of vintage glass plates. A few noted select images are magic lantern slides made by the Charles Beseler Co. in or after 1905. My deepest appreciation goes to Sheila Benedict for her help with historical references on many central missions. Many up-to-date mission photographs featured in "California Missions Past and Present: Touring El Camino Real" are from my visits to each area. Special appreciation is given to Amy Perryman, associate publisher at Arcadia Publishing, for her guidance through the process and believing we could make it possible.

I am truly pleased this book's release coincides with the 300th anniversary year of Fr. Junípero Serra's birth. Miguel Josep Serra (Junípero was his chosen religious name) was born on November 24, 1713, in Petra, Majorca, one of the Balearic Islands, located some 150 miles off the coast of the Spanish mainland.

INTRODUCTION

The earliest California missions had been constructed simply of mud, grass, and tule reeds, as was the custom during Father Serra's years residing in the deep jungles of Mexico. Alta California's fifth settlement, Mission San Luis Obispo de Tolosa, was founded in honor of the famous Saint Louis of Toulouse, consecrated on September 1, 1772, as the first of Central California. El Camino Real, or "The Royal Road," had reached into uncharted regions of Alta California following Father Serra's famous journey to meet supply ships in San Diego and then on to appear before the viceroy in Mexico City. Father Serra founded the Mission San Luis Obispo in a low plain first discovered by Gaspar de Portolá and named by him "Valley of the Bears." Grizzly bears had been observed and the enormous omnivores left immense mounds pawed up from foraging feasts north of Santa Maria. This led to good fortune for several soldiers exploring for food for mission colonies over three critical months. Nine thousand pounds of bear meat were delivered by a single hunting party and fed several missions. Supply ships coming into San Diego's port were unwilling to sail north to the Monterey harbor in early mission years, necessitating sending supply lines over land by mule pack trains. Mission San Luis Obispo de Tolosa had first been left under a single friar, Fr. José Cavaller, with five soldiers and two converted Baja Indians. This practice also helped to establish new *estancias*, or stations, providing a small adobe church and quarters at nearby *rancherias*. Father Serra's initial vision included a single Channel mission near the presidio in Santa Barbara, but eventually several manifested, including Missions San Buenaventura, La Purísima, Santa Bárbara, and Santa Inés. By 1774, Mission San Luis Obispo de la Tolosa had already survived three fires set by unfriendly natives as flaming arrows were shot directly into the adobe's dry thatched roofing in the day's hot sun. The mission fathers readily replaced the tule roofing with fired clay tiles and adopted this system at all mission settlements. Mission San Luis Obispo established outlying *asistencias*, the largest named Santa Margarita, a sub-mission built in 1787 that became a prosperous outpost. Near the location of Mission San Luis Obispo and set on a high plateau above today's Cuesta grade, it served a large concentration of Chumash Indians. The mission's impressive stone foundations are still visible centuries later, but they were incorporated beneath the roof of a modern hay barn decades ago. The asistencia contained a chapel, altar, living quarters for the majordomo, storage areas for harvests, and lodging for travelers. By 1804, the neophyte faithful at Mission San Luis Obispo had recorded 2,000 baptisms and over 1,000 deaths. The mission's settlement grew in both dimensions and productivity, and by 1820, native neophytes trained by Spanish craftsmen tended flourishing industries in agricultural trade. Over the years, Mission San Luis Obispo was elevated as one of six annual retreats that served all missionaries.

Father Serra's ninth mission, founded on Easter Sunday 1782 and consecrated as Mission San Buenaventura in honor of the Italian Franciscan Saint Bonaventure (1218–1274), became the first Channel mission. As a second link in this chain, Mission Santa Bárbara became the last dying wish of Father Serra's life. After a long awaited approval, Gov. Felipe de Neve agreed to send needed missionaries to serve the California mission colonies from Mexico City's Franciscan College of San Fernando. Father Serra had completed his life's work and retired to Carmel, living only two years more. Fr. Francisco Palóu, a longtime friend, companion, and biographer, became mission president briefly, then retired to Mexico following the demise of Father Serra in 1784. Father

Palóu recommended a new visionary, Fr. Fermín de Francisco Lasuén, mission president of Baja California, to follow as third president. Father Lasuén would found nine missions during the next decade. Mission Santa Bárbara's first church had been built of adobe brick with red clay tile roofing at the Santa Barbara presidio and was dedicated on December 4, 1786, by Father Lasuén. Mission Santa Bárbara's existing massive stone face and Spanish Moorish-style fountain were completed in 1820 and were rebuilt in 1950; the second tower was completed in 1831. Devastating earthquakes occurred in 1812 and 1925, greatly affecting Mission Santa Bárbara's structure and requiring major restoration. By 1842, by a decree of Pope Gregory XVI for a bishop as head of all the Californias, Fr. Garcia Diego was installed as head of the Baja and Alta California churches, residing at Mission Santa Bárbara. Mission San Carlos Borromeo del Rio Carmelo had been abandoned, and the "Queen of the Missions," Mission Santa Bárbara, withstood the transition to Mexican laws. The mission remained continually active and home to Franciscan padres, building its esteemed church archive and library. The adjacent apostolic college and historic adobe buildings housed a monastery training Franciscans and was completed in 1856. The Colegio Franciscano, a boys' school, opened in 1868. In 1901, St. Anthony's six buildings, integrated by a series of arcades, a cloister, a courtyard, and a patio, had been built adjacent to the mission complex to the north.

Father Lasuén founded the 11th mission in December 1787 and named it Mission La Purísima Concepción in honor of the Immaculate Conception of Mary the Most Pure. The original mission site, begun in 1788, was completed in 1791 and damaged by the earthquake of 1812, leveling all of the adobe buildings to the ground. The elaborate complex was rebuilt just four miles away in the Valley of the Watercress, and today's important replica stands completely restored as part of the California State Historic Parks system. The chain was expanded by Father Lasuén with the founding of Mission San Miguel, Arcángel, the 19th mission, in July 1797, connecting all northern missions on El Camino Real. Northeast of Santa Barbara, in the fertile Santa Ynez River Valley, Old Mission Santa Inés was established in September 1804 to continue the heritage of the Franciscans' central Alta California missions. Each mission featured distinct water systems for increasing populations, and the chain connected a diversity of Indian-run industries. A fire at Mission La Purísima Concepción in 1806 consumed large stores of wool, cloth, leather, and harvested grain, and a larger church was completed in 1816 at today's existing location. The mission's end came with transition to Mexico's rule, and the rebuilt Mission La Purísima fell under siege in 1823 when native riots were incited by a widespread revolt that spread from nearby missions. Rebels at the Mission La Purísima used the tools of their trades to build a fort to mount Spanish cannons and aim them at the Spanish soldiers. Six Spaniards and 17 Indians were left dead before this uprising was quelled by the Monterey presidio's militia, which arrested the leaders over the next month. The indigenous populations of Island Chumash, Barbareño, Salinan, and Yokuts were promised rewards of property after granting full rights beyond the status of neophyte. The mission fathers' magnetic pull and their monumental church settlements were closely guarded by soldiers and created obvious cultural differences that were viewed by natives outside the system as a deception against their familial and spiritual brethren.

TRANSITION TO STATEHOOD

After victory in its war for independence, Mexico by 1821 began instituting secularized laws aimed at dissolving the missionaries' power. All payments and supplies to soldiers and the missions were cut off. Padres were subjected to making contributions to the military, and secularization ultimately forced them to sell off church livestock, properties, and buildings and to permanently end their posts. In the year of California's statehood, 1850, the monumental mission buildings' legacy had begun to fade, and towns and spectacular cities had grown in their wake. Ranchers and *vaqueros* had entered the mission properties during a lawless period after neophyte Indians had been guaranteed property rights. In 1846, the American flag was raised over Monterey. A declaration followed that dispossessed all owners of property sold by Mexican governor Pío Pico. Loss of mission culture left the Indians and their families disbanded with little left of their ancestral homes or any promise of a future.

One

THE VALLEY OF HUNGRY BEARS

MISSION SAN LUIS OBISPO DE TOLOSA

Governor Portolá wandered through La Cañada de los Osos during his first land expedition and discovered a population of grizzly bears feasting in the tule marshes at their favorite feeding grounds. A hunting party spent three months living on bear meat, delivering 25 mule pack trains to the starving colonies. The site was chosen by Father Serra on September 1, 1772, to establish his fifth mission, San Luis Obispo de Tolosa, named for Saint Louis of Toulouse. (Author's collection.)

A magic lantern image from 1906 shows several makeshift additions to the church and mission buildings made around 1859. By 1868, the buildings had been covered with wood siding and shingles, and a wall was erected in the open portico of the monastery. An out-of-character, wood-framed, New England–style steeple was set atop the roof. (Author's collection.)

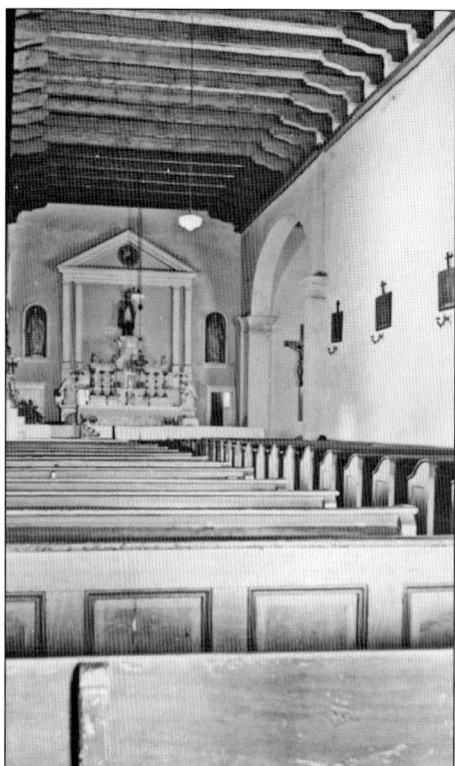

Mission San Luis Obispo de Tolosa's church nave and altar are pictured around 1936. Once restored, the mission was used as a parish church. Tradesmen from Spain had been the master architects of the missions. Under the direction of the Franciscans, most were constructed as adobe buildings at the outset of earliest settlements. During Father Serra's lifetime, buildings of mud, brushwood, and straw using timber framing and thatch roofing were common on El Camino Real. The friars experienced both friendly and unfriendly native inhabitants, and fires were set to several of the mission buildings' dry thatch roofs during the early days. Fired clay tiles were introduced to replace all of the missions' flammable roofing to avoid this type of attack.

The entrance to Mission San Luis de Tolosa is pictured around 1938, after the removal of redwood siding to help preserve it. The authentic restoration of the columns and monastery had been completed by this time. The sixth mission had been founded on September 1, 1772, by Fr. Junípero Serra and was first tended by Fr. José Cavaller with two Baja Indians and several soldiers. Father Cavaller died in 1789, and Fr. Miguel Gómez was appointed to take his place. By 1844, all neophytes were freed under secular laws.

This interior view of the Mission San Luis Obispo is from after 1936. Rebuilt according to early sketches, the original plain altar remained intact with five wooden statues, including one of Saint Louis, bishop of Toulouse, patron of the mission. Several earthquakes necessitated that the building be fully reinforced in 1934. The mission shared the distinction with Mission San Buenaventura of having a second nave extending the church at a right angle.

11

The adobe walls of Mission San Luis Obispo are six feet thick at their base, originally set on adobe mortar and fieldstones. Walls of adobe brick were plastered inside and out, then whitewashed. An early roadway below the colonnade's square openings is four feet lower at the original level.

The early baptismal font from Mission San Luis Obispo, made of hammered copper, was used by Father Serra to begin spiritual lives after neophyte conversions. Among the most cherished relics are original records of baptisms by Father Serra and written by his hand. Other records and artifacts include candlesticks, paintings, tools, original rough chapel benches, books, and vestments that were stored at the mission over the centuries. (Southwest Museum of the American Indian Collection.)

The extension of the chapel and several adjoining buildings surround the original monastery garden and grapevines. Fr. Luis Antonio Martínez spent 34 years at Mission San Luis Obispo, and during a brief period after 1832, protection came to the mission from Franciscan fathers of Mexican descent from the College of Guadelupe de Zacatecas, who filled the void of ministering to a dying culture. Ultimately, all mission adobe structures began to crumble throughout the system, often suffering from earthquake damage.

GENERAL JOHN C. FREMONT
AND HIS COMMAND OF
430 MEN
OF THE NAVY BATTALION
OF MOUNTED RIFLEMEN
ENCAMPED
NEAR THIS SITE
DECEMBER 14-18, 1846,
ON THEIR MARCH, WHICH ENDED
THE MEXICAN REGIME
IN CALIFORNIA.

ERECTED 1930 BY
SAN LUIS OBISPO
SCHOOL CHILDREN, NATIVE DAUGHTERS
AND
HISTORY AND LANDMARKS SECTION
OF THE MONDAY CLUB.

This view from 1936 was taken on Chorro Street after many restorations were made to bring the building back to an authentic design. Earthquakes had occurred in 1832 and 1868, destroying many of the mission's features. These were later remodeled to preserve the mission according to the original design.

This monument honors Gen. John C. Frémont, who surrounded the mission settlement in 1846, ending the occupation of Mexican insurrectionists. Many Californios living there were vaqueros, who swarmed into Alta California, aided by secularization laws, to take advantage of the rich cattle lands. Secularization of daily life, directed at taking away the power held by the missions, ultimately caused most to fall into complete demise. After 1859, all church and mission buildings were returned to the church by the US government. (Author's collection.)

Pensive moments were spent on scriptures as well as extensive recording from the early founding days and the study of native translations to reach new converts. Seated in this photograph is Father José around 1899. After the mission's last baptism was added in writing by the last Franciscan father, Fr. Ramon Abella, in 1841, the mission fell into disrepair. (Southwest Museum of the American Indian Collection.)

The church is at the rear of the interior quadrangle; the sacristy door entering the church nave is visible to the left of the tree. Fr. José Martinez, a jovial friar, was well known for his character in the Helen Hunt Jackson novel *Ramona*, with demonstrations of ducks, geese, turkeys, and chickens set up by mission neophytes in the courtyard to entertain the visiting Gen. Felipe Moreno and his new bride; the friar's poultry was driven past the couple in a procession lasting over an hour, to everyone's delight.

The largest bell in the wooden steeple weighed nearly 400 pounds and was inscribed "Manuel Vargas me fecit-Lima-Mision D. Sn Luis Obispo—De la Nueba California—Ano D. 1818." (Southwest Museum of the American Indian Collection.)

Grapevines and olive and pomegranate trees descended from those planted by the first friars still grow within the gardens of the mission. (Southwest Museum of the American Indian Collection.)

Recently rediscovered, this glass plate negative of 1928 depicts Mission San Luis Obispo's garden within the mission quadrangle and patio, grape arbors, and a complex of buildings adjacent to the church building. (Author's collection.)

At the mission property around 1928, a stone padre's kitchen near the garden portrays a simple architectural style from the past. The building is preserved today as a youth center and is located in the mission quadrangle. (Author's collection.)

A photograph from 1899 shows the main door of Mission San Luis Obispo and carved papal crests, delicate leaf-like tracings thought to be as old as the first mission. In 1870, Fr. John Harnett, the pastor, carefully removed a wood covering over the doors to expose the original design. The age and decay of the decorative lime plaster exterior over its brick and fieldstone walls is evident. (Southwest Museum of the American Indian Collection.)

By 1868, the structures had been rebuilt with wood siding, and an uncharacteristic New England–style steeple had been added. Fr. John Hartnett recognized the importance of using original plans for an accurate restoration of the mission at the beginning of the 20th century, an ongoing process that has lasted over many years.

The massive stone walls of Mission San Luis Obispo's Santa Margarita de Cortona Asistencia, a sub-mission, remained standing but were covered over in modern times, with a hay barn enclosing them. The three-foot-thick stone walls measured approximately 40 feet by 140 feet and were near adjoining grain fields that were prosperous through 1840, after all missions were in decline, abandoned, or sold. (Southwest Museum of the American Indian Collection.)

A vintage view from the beginning of the 20th century shows Santa Margarita de Cortona Asistencia's massive stone walls. As a sub-mission, it was a stop between San Luis Obispo de Tolosa and points north, with a chapel and monastery located on a high plateau at the top of the Cuesta grade. After 1840, this asistencia became private property, and public access to its buildings has remained limited. (Southwest Museum of the American Indian Collection.)

Santa Margarita de Cortona Asistencia had several nearby adobe buildings built by an unknown master stonemason with walls and arches of brick and stone. The setting comprised nearly 17,000 agricultural acres along the rich bottomland of the Salinas River used for extensive cattle grazing in later days. (Southwest Museum of the American Indian Collection.)

The walls of the Santa Margarita de Cortona Asistencia were incorporated in modern times into a large hay barn, fully enclosing them. This served to preserve what remained of the old building. Today it is a private tour attraction. (Southwest Museum of the American Indian Collection.)

After 1840, Rancho Santa Margarita lands were deeded to ranchers through large title grants of the Mexican government for secularized residential and business use. This original sketch made by Alfred Robinson in 1834, from *Life of California*, shows the exterior of the chapel shortly after being taken from the church.

The Works Progress Administration (WPA) plan from 1937 carries notes for architects recording the mission's structural condition and measurements. In the remarks, the floors, ceilings, stencils, and roofing have been noted as repaired, changed, or covered up. The survey eventually led the way to an authentic reversal of its deficiencies in the following years.

Two

SHORES OF SERENITY
MISSION SAN BUENAVENTURA

Mission Santa Buenaventura was long planned by Father Serra to reach the friendly natives of the Santa Barbara Channel and complete the first of several settlements reaching indigenous populations of the region. Established by Father Serra on March 31, 1782, and dedicated on Easter Sunday, the mission was the last of nine he founded during his lifetime. A cross was raised on a hill directly to the rear of the church, visible by land and sea. Today's church is located on the site of the stone church dedicated in 1809 and in use until an earthquake in 1812 left severe damage to the front and bell tower. By 1816, the mission building was reconstructed and all the interior woodwork replaced. (Author's collection.)

Father Serra brought Fr. Pedro Benito Cambón to help found Mission San Buenaventura and left Father Cambón in charge. Father Serra himself wrote the first pages of the baptismal records, although few natives were willing to join. The natives' trades of beads and trinkets helped build the structures of the settlement at first. The new church was destroyed by fire after 10 years, and the building existing today was completed in 1809. (Southwest Museum of the American Indian Collection.)

Among the early relics at Mission Buenaventura, a finely carved pulpit and canopy projecting from the side wall have been preserved over centuries. (Southwest Museum of the American Indian Collection.)

The richly enshrined altar holds many early artifacts that the church has held in safekeeping. As the Spanish missions fell into disrepair and neglect, the friars stored many vestments, liturgical items, and manuscripts at missions least affected by secularization, including Mission Santa Bárbara. (Southwest Museum of the American Indian Collection.)

The namesake of the mission, Saint Bonaventure was a legendary 13th-century Italian Franciscan friar whose works of philosophy and theology have been read over the centuries. He became an important minister-general of the Franciscan Order, maintaining a traditional and simplistic path of austerity. (Southwest Museum of the American Indian Collection.)

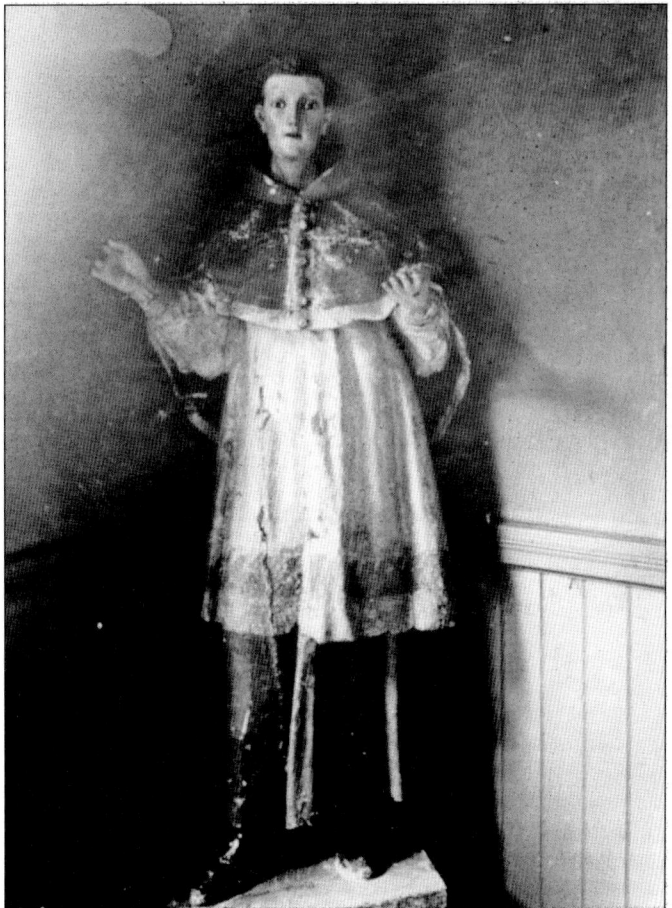

A photograph of the side entrance of Mission San Buenaventura taken near the beginning of the 20th century reveals the decorative Spanish-Moorish influenced relief designs with corniced pilasters framing the arched doorway and decorative entablature. The original "River of Life" pattern carved on the wooden doors was a native design feature carried over at many California missions. (Southwest Museum of the American Indian Collection.)

Candlesticks of silver and other relics were packed into a cave, some buried for a month, after reports that the pirate Hyppolyte de Bouchard, a Frenchman sailing under the Portuguese flag, was sighted along the channel coast in 1818. His plundering of the Alta California coastline struck fear into residents, who avoided him by retreating to the interior. (Southwest Museum of the American Indian Collection.)

A truly unusual artifact left at Mission San Buenaventura from 1782 is a bell of carved wood wrapped with rawhide. Mission fathers made do with a bell of wood before real bells could be purchased. This bell would make a simple hollow ring. (Southwest Museum of the American Indian Collection.)

In this rear view, Mission San Buenaventura's fully tiled quadrangle is centered in and surrounded by the growing town of Ventura during the late 1870s. (Southwest Museum of the American Indian Collection.)

Father Serra led his party to the shores of the Santa Barbara Channel, jubilant to find camp near a site the explorer Gov. Gaspar de Portolá had discovered during his first journey to the interior of Alta California. Portolá had named it La Asunción de Nuestra Señora. A large gathering of 70 soldiers and families had been recruited, and Gov. Felipe de Neve, displayed in full regalia, arrived with a guard of Monterey soldiers. The Mission San Buenaventura was consecrated on March 31, 1782, by Father Junípero Serra. (Southwest Museum of the American Indian Collection.)

The richly decorated church of Mission San Buenaventura is pictured and contains many works of religious art. The church was repaired between 1878 and 1895 by Fr. Ciprian Rubio, by covering the beamed ceiling and the tile floors with wood, whitewashing the walls, and replacing the window with stained glass. The church was authentically restored in 1957, removing the previous alterations. (Southwest Museum of the American Indian Collection.)

A vintage postcard shows the side entry to the church and fountain at Mission San Buenaventura. The earliest explorer for Spain, Juan Rodríguez Cabrillo, had landed nearby on his first discovery of Alta California in 1542, naming it El Pueblo Canoas, or "Town of the Canoes." The impressive boats of tule and planks he had observed were very seaworthy and capable of carrying 15 to 20 passengers. (Author's collection.)

Behind Mission San Buenaventura are the grounds of the quadrangle, pictured here around 1930. Later, the mission's courtyard was fully restored to its former beauty and surrounded by lush gardens.

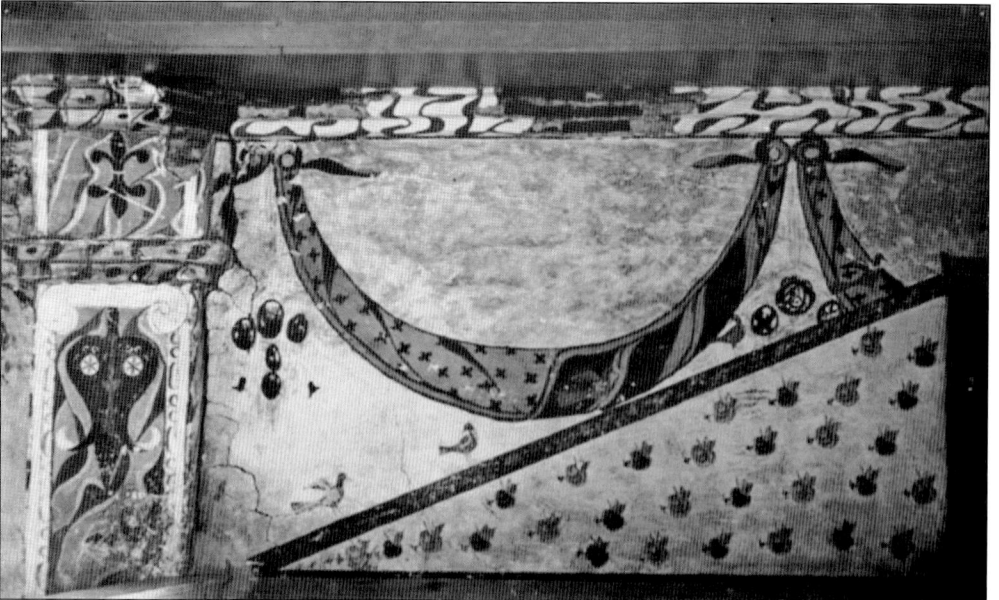

The Island Chumash used many mineral substances to create the brilliant colors seen in their art. Several native finds included cinnabar, diatomaceous earth, burned graphite, charcoal, and natural asphalt tars. (Southwest Museum of the American Indian Collection.)

This old wooden chair, reportedly used by Father Serra, is revered as an early relic at Mission San Buenaventura. (Southwest Museum of the American Indian Collection.)

Many iron tools were made by talented neophytes trained by Spanish blacksmiths forging utensils for cooking or digging the rugged soils and gardens. (Southwest Museum of the American Indian Collection.)

A photograph from the turn of the 20th century reveals Ventura roads and meandering coaches and carriages along the original El Camino Real, the main roadway passing north and south.

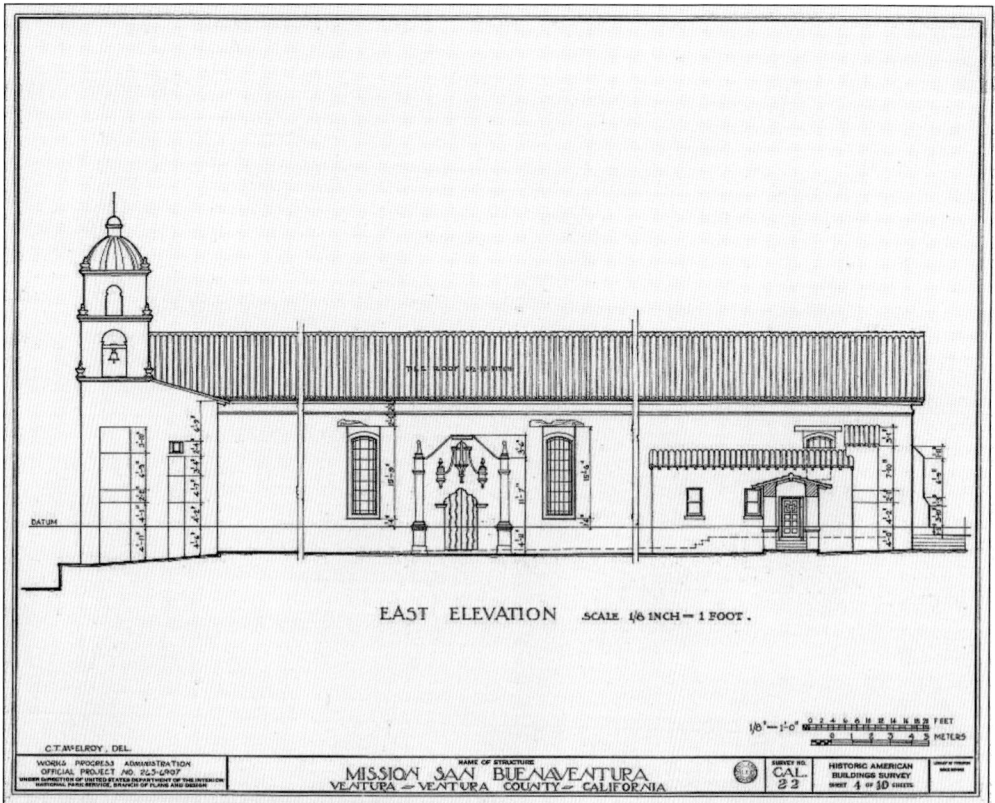

EAST ELEVATION SCALE 1/8 INCH = 1 FOOT.

This elevation drawing of Mission San Buenaventura was used about 1930 for artists of the Index of American Design, a specific talent pool to restore authentic designs and building details from the mission era. All California mission restorations have benefited from this living resource.

Three

THE GOLDEN AGE
OF THE MISSIONS
MISSION SANTA BÁRBARA

The Santa Barbara Channel, honored by Sebastián Vizcaíno's expedition from 1602, and its beautiful harbor, had been first sighted in 1542 by Juan Rodríguez Cabrillo, discoverer of Alta California. Due to rough seas, Cabrillo anchored on a nearby island across from Santa Barbara later called San Miguel. Charting stormy windswept waters to the north, Cabrillo returned to San Miguel Island unexpectedly; he was wounded and died there in January 1543 after a fatal injury to his arm aboard ship. Mission Santa Bárbara, founded in 1786 by Fr. Fermín de Francisco Lasuén, emerged from an active presidio and settlement. Earthquake destruction in 1812 and 1814 would demand immediate reconstruction of the mission, completed by 1820 under the master builder José Antonio Ramirez. Before this construction, three adobe churches were built, each larger than the last, to accommodate a growing population at the mission. (Author's collection.)

The presidio site is where Father Serra had accompanied Gov. Felipe de Neve and Capt. José Francisco Ortega with 50 soldiers in 1782, founding California's fourth military pueblo. Mission Santa Bárbara had been planned before his death and was later founded in 1786 in honor of Saint Barbara, who lived in the Roman Empire at the end of the 3rd century. (Southwest Museum of the American Indian Collection.)

This view from 1936 shows the sculpted *lavanderia* (laundry basin) at the front entrance to the convento. The Moorish-style fountain of 1808 was connected to two large dams that provided drinking water, cleaned by straining it through charcoal beds within a stone filter building, then piped to the mission through a series of fired clay tiles. A sculpted bear spouts water into the basin. (Southwest Museum of the American Indian Collection.)

Between 1815 and 1820, José Antonio Ramirez, a master carpenter and stonemason from Spain, designed and built the church and convent of Mission Santa Bárbara, the 10th mission in Alta California. A large tower projected upwards with a distinct stepped design, and a second tower was added in 1831. Both were slightly toppled by a 1925 earthquake and immediately rebuilt. (Author's collection.)

Photographed in 1937, artifacts from the mission era included an early ox-driven *carreta*, or Spanish-style cart, with the laundry basin to the rear where water flows to a brick basin from the mission fountain above. (Author's collection.)

The graceful Mission Santa Bárbara as depicted in this postcard has stood impressively for two centuries. By 1807, over 1,700 mission Indians were living inside the community, and over 250 adobe huts surrounded the mission grounds. (Author's collection.)

By 1872, changes had been made to the mission. Within the 1820 church, the original pulpit was taken down and altars had been dismantled and replaced. The communion railing and steps were replaced in the church, and redwood wainscoting was added to the bottom six feet of the church walls, covering original frescos. A wooden floor had been laid over the original tile floor of the church.

The church door of carved wood was made by Indian labor in 1820 in a pattern called "River of Life," effortlessly resting under the support of its massive three-foot-thick lintel. This pattern had been duplicated at several missions and had meaningful decorative additions given by the Chumash as combined cultural art interpreting their understanding of the world. The Spanish, duplicating successes from previous settlements in Baja, introduced friendly Indians into Alta California as ambassadors for the missionaries, allowing colonization to ultimately establish missions.

A c. 1906 magic lantern slide produced by the Beseler Co. depicts an iconic image of a solemn friar in a contemplative reverent state at the mission. Friars from Mission Santa Bárbara were subjects of postcards and media more than all other missions due to its beautiful gardens, stone walls, and longevity, making it a star tourist attraction in California. (Author's collection.)

Surviving over generations through natural disasters, the bells of Mission Santa Bárbara included this one from 1797. Miraculously, when the tower toppled in the 1925 earthquake, the remaining parts held two bells undamaged after the tremors. (Southwest Museum of the American Indian Collection.)

The *campanario* was crushed under its own weight after the 1925 earthquake. Tremors continued to greatly affect the mission. (Southwest Museum of the American Indian Collection.)

In this photograph from 1899, posed within the campanario at Mission Santa Bárbara, the friar was one who continuously provided the care of the Franciscan Order to California's Queen of the Missions. In 1842, Mission Santa Bárbara was appointed headquarters for the first Roman Catholic bishop of California, Fr. Garcia Diego, celebrated with an installment of escort troops, officials, and a kneeling multitude of devout citizens on January 11, 1842. (Southwest Museum of the American Indian Collection.)

Chumash Indian designs brought by neophyte Indians were often as intricate and delicate as they were colorful. This photograph shows the artistic complexity of the hand carving that made a simple choir railing into a work of art. (Southwest Museum of the American Indian Collection.)

Mission Santa Bárbara's cornerstone was laid in 1815, and during the next five years, the mission was continuously worked on. In 1817, Captain Wilcox, an Australian trader visiting the area on his ship *Traveller*, went across the channel to Santa Cruz Island, returning with enough hewn timbers to complete the mission's roof beams. (Author's collection.)

This vintage postcard depicts the damage caused to Mission Santa Bárbara in 1925 by the most severe earthquake in over a century. Severe earthquakes in the channel region had stopped the progress of explorer Gaspar de Portolá, governor of Baja, in 1770 during his land expedition to locate Monterey Bay. Badly frightened, the entire party had recorded several long-lasting, intense tremors but eventually proceeded to their destination. (Author's collection.)

Pres. Theodore Roosevelt visited Mission Santa Bárbara during his first term in 1903, two years after accompanying President McKinley's official visit as his vice president. This followed a previous visit by Pres. Benjamin Harrison. Also in 1903, Roosevelt met with John Muir, the great park preservationist, on his historic trip to Yosemite.

Blacksmithing was a trade brought from Spain to the missions along with other European skills used to maintain the settlements taking root in Alta California. Indigenous populations had been attracted to and fascinated by tools. Many mastered the use of iron tools and agricultural implements.

The 1925 earthquake leveled much of the town and ruptured a dam, flooding Sycamore Canyon near town. The first tremor at 6:00 a.m. seemed light but triggered two of the most severe tremors five minutes apart; aftershocks lasted for a week to a lesser degree. (Southwest Museum of the American Indian Collection.)

This dramatic view shows the decorated church interior at Mission Santa Bárbara before modern restorations. By 1911–1912, an interior renovation of the church occurred, the sanctuary was extended forward, and its floor was raised and replaced with new concrete. A new altar replaced the one of 1872. The wood flooring of 1872 was pulled up and replaced with tiles and red cement to resemble the original. Similarly, the redwood wainscoting of 1872 was removed and the original frescoes repainted. Other alterations to doors, woodwork, and altars were also made. The whole church interior received a fresh coat of paint. Outside of the church, the interior mission cloister garden was extensively redone. (Southwest Museum of the American Indian Collection.)

Relics of the carefully restored first altar at Mission Santa Bárbara include a hand-drawn choir manuscript. Musical art was greatly encouraged by the friars at many California missions with the use of European instruments and tablature. (Author's collection.)

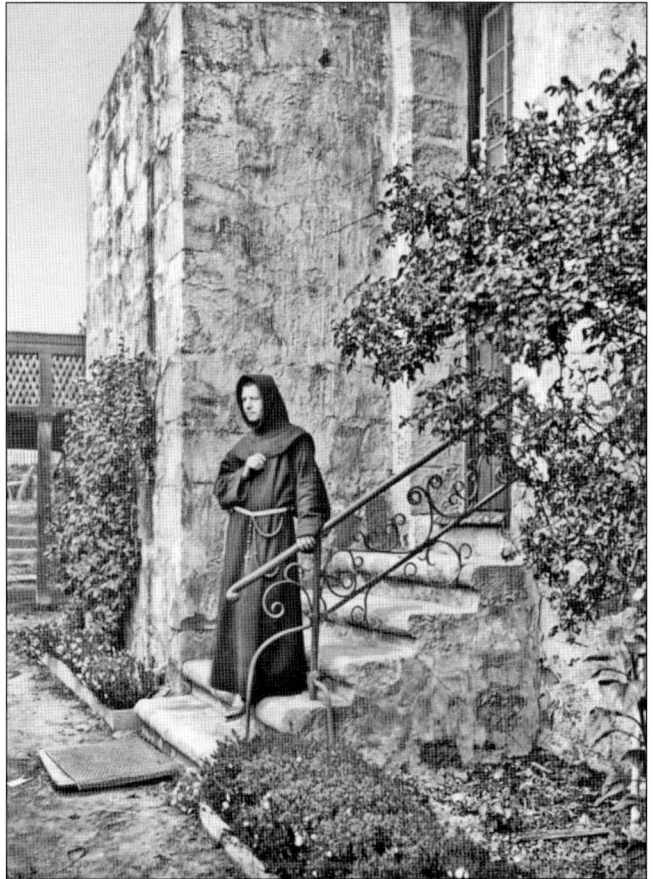

The tranquility of the monastic lifestyle led by the Franciscan monks is depicted in this photograph of Brother Odoricus. Mission Santa Bárbara was often the subject of early California postcards, as in this early photochrom print by Detroit Publishing.

A vintage photograph depicts Mission Santa Bárbara, established as the second "Channel Mission" and the first mission founded by Father Lasuén. It was one of three Alta California missions built from cut sandstone, along with the Royal Presidio Cathedral.

A conference in 1893 of convening missionaries at Mission Santa Bárbara included Fr. Joseph Jeremiah O'Keefe (right), overseer of Missions San Juan Capistrano and San Luis Rey. He was well known for preserving the venerable buildings from complete disrepair. (Southwest Museum of the American Indian Collection.)

The ancient image of the Thunderbird from Chumash art is featured on mission interiors. A labor of love carried the lore of historic Indian art and color to embellish the walls and ceilings, creating time capsules of early Native American art. After thousands of years in California, the Chumash were quick to learn the advantages of modernity, construction, industry, and agriculture, supporting the early mission cause. (Southwest Museum of the American Indian Collection.)

Mission Santa Bárbara is highly romanticized as Alta California's "Queen of the Missions." Diversified cultures of indigenous Channel Chumash, Baja Californios, Franciscan padres, and Americans lived simultaneously at the mission with its active presidio and harbor. Planned by the Spanish Crown and aided by the Pious Fund, the four Channel Missions included Missions San Buenaventura, Santa Bárbara, La Purísima Concepción, and Santa Inés. The archives residing at Mission Santa Bárbara had been recorded and collected by Franciscan padres over centuries. This literature survives with early photography to support the work of the CCC during the New Deal, restoring the mission chain throughout the Golden State by implementing the application of the newly formed Index of American Design, a modern compendium of academia, artists, and researchers. (Author's collection.)

This 1960s postcard gives an aerial view of Mission Santa Bárbara and St. Anthony's seminary, built in 1901, and their classic architecture. (Author's collection.)

The carved Spanish Colonial mission doors and elaborate entry into the large chapel of the mission were recorded by the Historic American Building Survey during the 1930s at Mission Santa Bárbara. The stone facade was finished in 1820, and was refinished in 1950 after the 1925 earthquake. It was a masterwork of José Antonio Rameriz, mason and designer.

Arid coastal lands were natural for succulent gardens, easily supporting a thriving floral and agricultural base in the Santa Barbara area. Ellwood Cooper, an Australian, introduced many successful plants that were drought-resistant from that continent to Santa Barbara.

Saint Francis (1182–1226) was the patron saint of the Franciscan Order. This statue in the Mission Santa Bárbara courtyard shows him nurturing a dove, as he was able to commune with many different animals. It was his habit to invoke all birds, all animals, and all reptiles to praise and love their creator. Many times during Francis's life, he was recorded as speaking to the animals. A ravenous wolf was quelled after he famously spoke to the animal, urging it to make a pledge to remain peaceful with citizens previously terrorized by its ferocious hunting and disorder. The wolf would lie meekly at his feet in reverence. (Author's collection.)

This carreta, a Spanish oxcart, is tended by a friar at Mission Santa Bárbara. The equivalent of the modern tractor and truck, this allowed the missionaries to move their goods and materials handily. (Author's collection.)

This Australian fig tree, planted around 1910, stands within the mission's cemetery among nearly 4,000 Indian graves. Mission Santa Bárbara's success, if measured by neophyte conversions, exceeded many of its sister mission properties within the system. (Author's collection.)

The mission church windows illuminate the massive features with the glow of the southern sun. Fr. Narciso Durán spent time at Mission San Buenaventura, then became mission-president. Residing at Mission Santa Bárbara, he devoted 12 years to popular concerts, leading a performing orchestra of mission Indians playing European instruments. After a total of 40 years living in the province, his passing marked the end of the Spanish mission era. (Author's collection.)

The monastery kitchen from 1808 at Old Mission Santa Bárbara appears on a popular postcard. Coming from two reservoirs one-and-a-half miles from the mission, water supplied power for a gristmill built in 1806 and was fed along an open stone-lined flume to process oats, barley, wheat, and corn. (Author's collection.)

The shoemaker at Mission Santa Bárbara is working in 1899 at one of several industries the self-reliant friars had adopted to maintain the simplicity of their lifestyle and faith. (Southwest Museum of the American Indian Collection.)

The carreta remained as a valuable artifact in this photograph from 1937. It was an important vehicle used for transportation on El Camino Real and could haul heavy supplies to the Alta California colonies. (Southwest Museum of the American Indian Collection.)

The reception room's entryway projects an authentic feel of the spacious interior at Mission Santa Bárbara. This photograph from the beginning of the 20th century includes, carved on the door at right, a pattern visible at many missions called "River of Life." (Southwest Museum of the American Indian Collection.)

A close-up of the tabernacle's intricate features shows carved and painted devotee figures adorning the container of the Holy Ghost in the form of the blessed host and wine. (Southwest Museum of the American Indian Collection.)

A postcard view of the Mission Santa Bárbara entrance reveals the church's massive portico by the church's stone walls. Sandstone was quarried and brought to the site, a material used by only three other early California missions. Abalone shells provided a traditional slaked lime mix to bond the materials up to seven feet thick in archways.

An unusual postcard printed in Germany gives a view of the "old bathhouse," one of many old adobe or stone buildings that have disappeared over time. Mission Santa Bárbara's facade had been plastered like most brick, stone, and adobe buildings of the era. (Author's collection.)

Revealing the beautifully carved wooden statues of the reredos, the main altar had been reconstructed around 1876, but the original, smaller altar and tabernacle, along with other authentic relics, were acquired after the founding from the other missions and stored for safekeeping. (Author's collection.)

A padre, in pensive study at the mission garden courtyard, is depicted in a postcard from around 1960. Due to the importance they placed on literacy and recording daily activities, Mission Santa Bárbara was perhaps the most successful of all California missions guided by a long lineage of Franciscan friars. (Author's collection.)

The beautiful grounds at Mission Santa Bárbara remind one the mission's role in past centuries as an important port. Sailors and ships would arrive continuously from many ports of call, including in 1794 British navigator George Vancouver, who wrote extensively on his journey to the vibrant land. (Author's collection.)

An early postcard view taken north of Mission Santa Bárbara shows the surrounding Santa Ynez Mountains, through which extensive trails led high above towards nearby Mission Santa Inés in the Santa Ynez River valley.

Festive caballeros gather at a traditional Christmas commemoration at Mission Santa Bárbara, an example of activities that were part of the California missionary friars' lives during the secularized era. (Southwest Museum of the American Indian Collection.)

The treasures of Mission Santa Bárbara, kept safe over the years by Franciscan friars, included this altar and tabernacle supporting its highly carved devotee figures, a fine example of religious art from Europe influencing California and Mexico. (Southwest Museum of the American Indian Collection.)

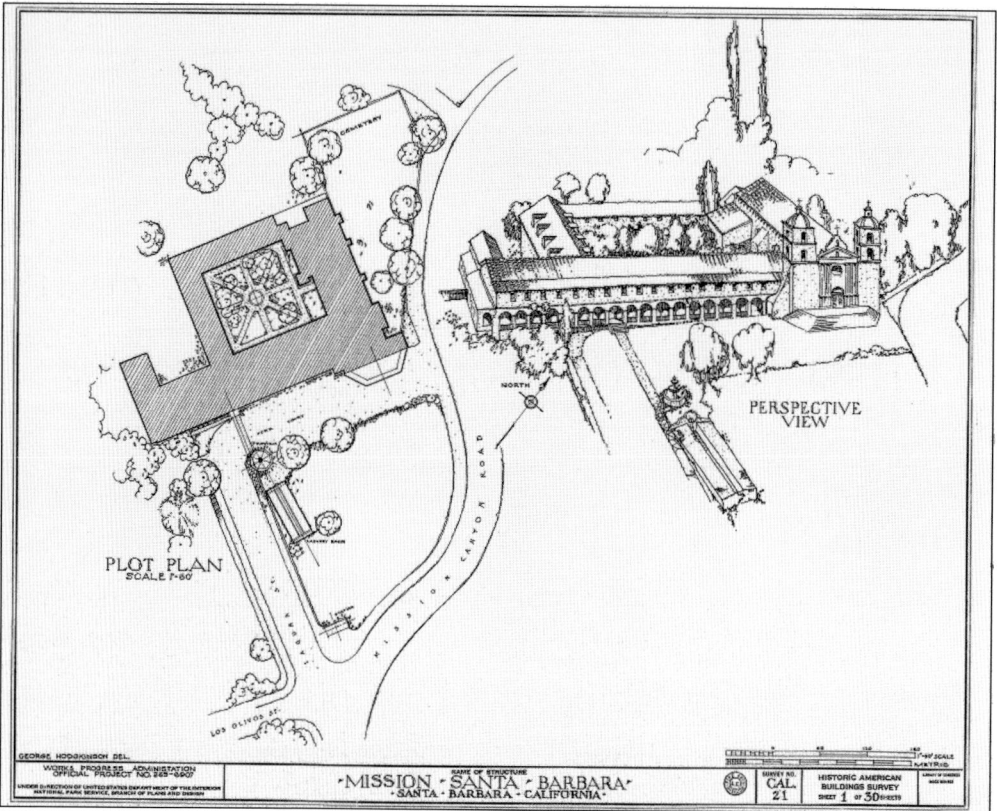

PLOT PLAN
SCALE 1=60

PERSPECTIVE VIEW

·MISSION·SANTA·BARBARA·
·SANTA·BARBARA·CALIFORNIA·

This Mission Santa Bárbara plot map was used about 1937. In 1865, the mission was restored 283 acres of its property when an effort to make the buildings more inhabitable was accomplished by Fr. Peter Wallischeck, who raised the old monastery wing roof to a second level.

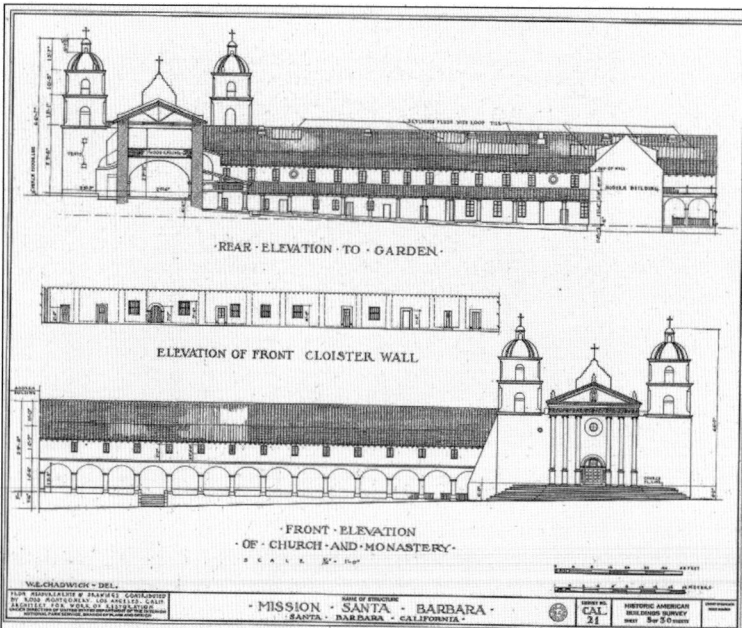

·REAR·ELEVATION·TO·GARDEN·

ELEVATION OF FRONT CLOISTER WALL

·FRONT·ELEVATION·
·OF·CHURCH·AND·MONASTERY·

·MISSION·SANTA·BARBARA·
·SANTA·BARBARA·CALIFORNIA·

This key elevation plan was used during CCC restorations around 1937. The drawings give a clear definition of the mission's architecture on paper and are held at the Library of Congress. They helped bring the right artisans and builders to complete the project.

Four

Utopian Time and Place
Mission La Purísima Concepción

This c. 1928 glass-plate image shows the Mission La Purísima Concepción de la Santísima Virgen María (Immaculate Conception of the Most Blessed Virgin Mary) and ruins that were overgrown after a century of neglect. The original adobe mission had been finished in 1802, four miles inland of the channel, and was founded by Fr. Fermín de Francisco Lasuén on the Feast of the Immaculate Conception, December 8, 1787. From the seasonal banks of Rio Santa Inés, it moved to the town of Lompoc after an earthquake in 1812 destroyed the original settlement. Both locations were serviced by the beloved Fr. Mariano Payéras until his death in 1823. (Author's collection.)

Mission La Purísima Concepción is the 11th in the chain and last of the Channel Missions. A distance from the main trails of modernity, the mission's restoration is evident in this photograph from 1940. It had by then become a California State Historic Park with 10 of the original buildings completed, including the church, shops, quarters, and blacksmith shop. (Author's collection.)

The California State Historic Park represents many original industries run by local Chumash Indians, who readily assimilated skills and crafts, adopting Spanish iron and steel tools. Many tools were made by their own hands. The long architectural footprint was unique among the quadrangle designs of most California mission settlements. (Author's collection.)

By the 1920s, a lone surviving table served passing motorists for picnics in the park-like area. This popular spot near the nine remaining monastery columns was soon added to the major reconstruction of Mission La Purisima Concepción after it was acquired by the California State Historic Parks system in 1935. (Anderson Family Collection.)

Wood forms allowed adobe bricks to be poured, dried, sun baked, and then set on their edges for reconstruction projects. Bricks used to build the mission's walls averaged 60 pounds each. Indian laborers spent days felling trees to make clearings and lumber, carrying stones from the river, and digging out open pits of adobe clay. Manufacturing, stockpiling, and transporting large quantities of supplies was necessary, and the padres learned how to speed this process for their enormous structures.

This 1905 image shows the south wall of Mission la Purisima Concepción's first site's church, built in 1803 but destroyed in the earthquake of 1812. The towering ruins of adobe, clay, rawhide, timber, and tule reeds attracted curiosity seekers, artists, photographers, and archeologists. Touring California's romantic scenery and wonders by automobile became a popular attraction. (Southwest Museum of the American Indian Collection.)

WPA workers are pictured painting and restoring the interior of Mission La Purísima Concepción in Lompoc, California, during the years from 1935 to 1941. (Southwest Museum of the American Indian Collection.)

Although the original design is unknown, Mission La Purísima Concepción's *espadaña* (bell tower) was restored with the first phase of rebuilding by the Civilian Conservation Corps. The job involved 200 stout individuals and not more than $6,000 in costs, by virtue of their manufacturing their own materials from 1935 to 1937. The project was the second largest of its kind in American history, next to Jamestown, Virginia. (Southwest Museum of the American Indian Collection.)

The Mission La Purísima Concepción ruins are pictured in 1910. Modern reconstruction used a small portion of the original church walls with nine brick piers of the east corridor and part of the adobe walls from the original structure of 1818. (Southwest Museum of the American Indian Collection.)

As hundreds of Chumash Indians, the local natives of the Santa Barbara Channel, were baptized into the church, they were taught by Spanish craftsmen and missionaries to labor and build the California missions. Soldiers had been quartered in buildings on the Mission La Purísima Concepción's property to see that the faithful Indians remained at work in the community. (Author's collection.)

A glass-plate photograph from 1928 depicts the stunning remains of the monastery's squared openings and the nine remaining pillars, an identifiable architectural feature of Mission La Purísima Concepción. Constructed by the master masons of the time, the columns and parts of the walls had defied a century of deterioration. (Author's collection.)

Remaining artifacts included two brick laundries and a brick cistern, each repaired to working order. Many thorough restorations at Mission La Purísima Concepción were carried out through the 1940s. (Southwest Museum of the American Indian Collection.)

From 1931, Mission La Purísima Concepción land acquisition began for a California State Historic Park commemorating the early settlement of Alta California by the Spanish Franciscan missionaries. Later, garden plants were brought from all the missions to plant here during the restoration, with many native plants blooming throughout the year. (Author's collection.)

In 1912, the ruins and columns of Mission La Purísima Concepción were a century old but remarkably resistant to age. The second church had been completed in 1815 and greatly affected by the Mexican secular laws. It soon fostered insurgent Indians who rebelled there, led by mission Indians from Santa Inés. It had been abruptly abandoned by 1836.

A classic postcard shows Mission La Purísima Concepción before the beginning of the 20th century, when it was still abandoned. The destruction of the first adobe mission church after the 1812 earthquake had prompted Father Payéras to relocate the church and mission, quelling the fears of the neophytes. The population of Chumash Indians at Mission La Purísima Concepción had increased to 1,000 by August 1815. The new church was completed with adobe brick and adobe mortar, burned brick, stone, and plastered-over walls and columns. (Author's collection.)

In ruins around 1912, Mission La Purísima Concepción required extensive restoration led by the Civilian Conservation Corps combined with county, state, and federal agencies. The historic reconstruction was one of the largest of its kind in America, requiring hundreds of specialized craftsmen and skilled builders to recreate an expansive complex of buildings.

The ruins at Mission La Purísima Concepción are pictured in 1904, after they had been abandoned for nearly 70 years. This residence building was often depicted in photographs. California's wet winter conditions made it difficult for rammed-earth adobe bricks to survive. (Southwest Museum of the American Indian Collection.)

The unique mission portico was built without arched openings and was distinguished by its squared architecture. The residence building had been rebuilt entirely of new materials using foundation rocks and a few exterior walls, with nine original piers used in the restoration. The foundations of three utility buildings, a blacksmith shop, palisade building, three neophyte buildings, a warehouse building, and an infirmary were uncovered. (Author's collection.)

As the largest reconstruction effort of its time in California, Mission La Purísima Concepción was largely completed in 1938, its restoration culminating in one of the best examples of early California Spanish Mission architecture to demonstrate the founding settlements of the state. It was rededicated by the Franciscan friars and blessed. It now serves as a historical park with living history reenactments and authoritative historians accessible for visitors. (Author's collection.)

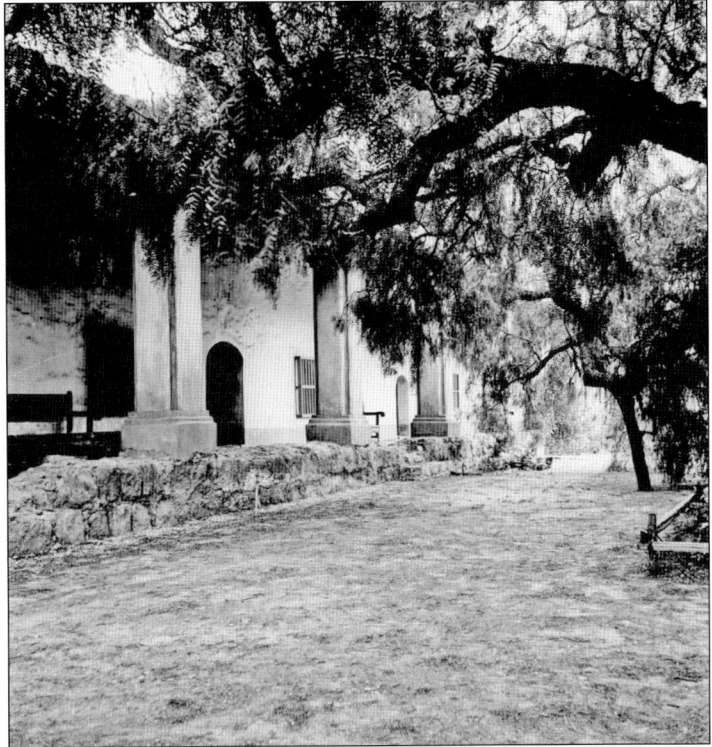

This south view of Mission La Purísima Concepción's church after restorations captures the exterior details completed in 1938. More upgrades were completed later in 1941. (Author's collection.)

This 1937 photograph taken by the Historic American Building Survey shows the completed residence building incorporating several original piers and columns.

The project to rebuild Mission La Purísima Concepción's complex on original footings began soon after the mission property had been acquired by the state in 1935. This photograph, taken for the Historic American Building Survey, records its recovery and the condition of the most important buildings.

A photograph from the turn of the century depicts the remaining wing of the convento that resisted final demise from wet weather after the beginning of the 20th century. Natives who had built the mission complex had taken several years to gather and manufacture the components of brick, stone, tile, and ingredients to make mortar and plaster. This gave way to a two-year construction period during which the massive complex was quickly assembled.

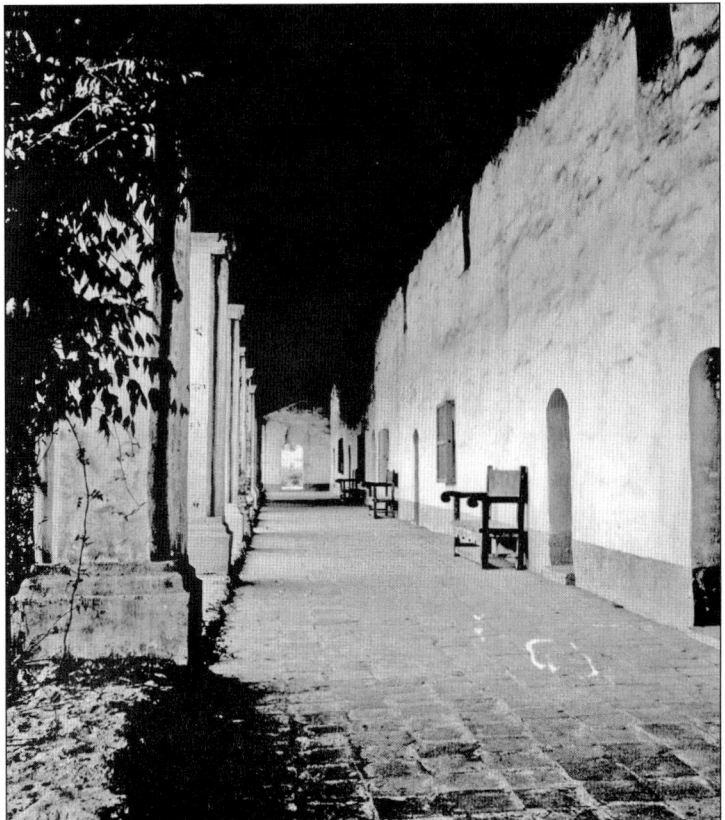

The squared openings to Mission La Purísima Conception's portico are a departure from the Roman arches used at many California missions. (Author's collection.)

The massive mission church greeted the first visitors to rediscover California's early history when the park opened in 1937. The renovations would take many more years to reach all of the 21 missions of El Camino Real. (Southwest Museum of the American Indian Collection.)

The west corridor of the utilities building is pictured in 1937 during reconstruction, prior to its roof installation. The sun casts dramatic patterns through the skeleton onto an old adobe wall. (Southwest Museum of the American Indian Collection.)

The Civilian Conservation Corps (CCC) continued the work of the reconstruction at Mission La Purísima Concepción's church. The men in this 1937 photograph are using an authentic adze, a tool for squaring timbers into usable beams. (Southwest Museum of the American Indian Collection.)

The chapel nave was completely redecorated by skill artisans between 1935 and 1941. Fr. Mariano Payéras, in service over 19 years, used craftsmen and trained neophytes to complete many ornate designs. (Southwest Museum of the American Indian Collection.)

Gatherings brought together worker groups taking part in the restoration on many levels, including personnel from California State Historic Parks, CCC and WPA federal programs, archeologists, historians, and qualified artists. (Southwest Museum of the American Indian Collection.)

A vintage postcard view from 1940 shows the pastoral setting that kept Mission La Purísima Concepción in pristine condition at this serene spot. Located four miles inland from Lompoc, the original mission site was moved to a more fertile location where it became a major modern-day restoration project. (Author's collection.)

After restoration, jubilant friars from the Franciscan Order are pictured at the church entry in commemoration of the newly restored mission church. (Southwest Museum of the American Indian Collection.)

The completed restoration of the fountain of Mission La Purísima Concepción is pictured in 1937, with gardens replanted around the mission. Many native and European plants were adopted after the mission's founding. Wheat, olives, peaches, and grapes were grown. The cultural assimilation of the natives and the newcomers had created successful enterprises, including raising cattle and horses, under the management of the Franciscan friars. (Southwest Museum of the American Indian Collection.)

This turn-of-the-century photograph depicts a common condition throughout the historic mission system in California. Often, after the roofing tiles caved in and were lost, the timbers and adobe then declined into irreversible ruin. Mission La Purísima Concepción had endured an extended period of neglect and abandonment, leaving behind a series of decayed buildings. (Southwest Museum of the American Indian Collection.)

Five

THE MIDDLE WAY

MISSION SAN MIGUEL, ARCÁNGEL

Mission San Miguel, Arcángel, the 16th mission, was central to all mission locations and one of three founded in 1797 established by Father Lasuén. The location was directly along El Camino Real near adequate water sources, and the region is midway along the important passage from southern to northern California. The mission baptized 15 native children the day of its founding and reached a maximum of 1,169 neophyte converts by 1804. (Author's collection.)

The original *enramada* or mission of natural brushwood predated the first mission named for Saint Michael the Archangel, and it was quickly replaced by an adobe church in 1798, constructed under the direction of Fr. Buenaventura Sitjar and Fr. Antonio Horra. The first structure was 28 feet by 34 feet and had an earth-covered roof. The settlement had been built as a quadrangle filled in with adobe hut housing for neophytes, workshops, and a granary near the mission. (Author's collection.)

The stone espadaña, an architectural feature standing at the center of the mission building, held three bells. The present church was begun in 1816 and completed in 1818. By 1834, it was among the last of the missions to be secularized; the property was sold in 1845, then returned to the church in 1859. It was occupied by a variety of residents until reoccupied again by a resident priest assigned to Mission San Miguel in 1878, when the mission parish was established. (Author's collection.)

The masonry espadaña is unique among all the missions, as it uses a stepped stone archway with three arched windows for the bells. As an interesting historical note, each mission was granted $1,000 by the Spanish crown–backed Pious Fund to establish the settlement.

The reredos behind the altar and the stations of the cross along the decorated walls, with the art directed by Estéban Munras in 1821, have been important features for which Mission San Miguel, Arcángel is known. Many early carved statues were created by the neophytes, who also partook in a range of diverse industries to sustain the mission culture.

The corridor of 16 arches directly corresponds to Mission San Miguel, Arcángel's place in the lineage of the Alta California chain. The mission settlements were positioned outside the region to give padres the ability to venture out from time to time, seeking conversions. Over 10 years, from 1807 to 1817, Fr. Juan Cabot conducted baptisms near Lake Tulare. He ventured to a nearby tribe in the middle of a dispute after one native life and two Spanish horses were lost. He reported that parallel mission settlements would potentially benefit in expanding the existing California chain. (Southwest Museum of the American Indian Collection.)

The original bell of 1800 survived through the years and was hung within the archways after 1859, when the mission was once again overseen by the Franciscans. (Southwest Museum of the American Indian Collection.)

Mission San Miguel Archangel
San Miguel, California

This real-photo postcard of Mission San Miguel, Arcángel was made by well-known California photographer Burton Frasher around 1955. He recorded many of California's historic features and parks. The mission was situated directly off today's US Highway 101 in San Miguel. (Author's collection.)

The enormous bell in this photograph was recast from original bells in San Francisco in 1888 and hung within a frame of wooden supports in the mission courtyard. It is reported to weigh 2,500 pounds. It was traditionally sounded three times each day. (Southwest Museum of the American Indian Collection.)

This photograph shows the turn-of-the-century Mission San Miguel, Arcángel. The mission settlement was located near the junction of the Nacimiento and Salinas Rivers and centered in flat fertile lands that created agricultural prosperity. It completed the chain to northern missions.

A view from the choir loft above portrays the ancient chapel nave; 28 beams span the full width, and each sits on large rough wooden corbels. The hewn wood was brought from Cambria by neophytes, attached through the sides of the walls, then fastened by large wooden spikes. The natives contributed decorative artwork on balconies, doors, and archways; a life-size Saint Michael the Archangel, the patron of the mission, stands centered above the altar.

The reredos at Mission San Miguel, Arcángel has elaborately designed panels separated by pillars finished with mottled designs made to resemble marble. The background of the three panels is framed with paintings of green foliage with vivid red flowers. The central figure of Saint Michael is a six-foot-high carved wooden statue. The artwork within the nave remains one of the true wonders of the mission era.

This view of the entry doors shows the church accumulating intense morning light, as missions had been designed to illuminate during specific services on special seasonal occasions.

Before roof tiles had been made, in 1806, the mission was severely damaged by a fire that brought down part of the chapel walls and two rows of tule-covered workshops holding a stockpile of wool, hides, cloth, tools, and implements. In addition, 6,000 pounds of wheat were destroyed. Other missions contributed to those that were hit by disasters, and thousands of tiles were stockpiled with help from fired kilns. Fr. Juan Martinez guided the reconstruction of 1816, stockpiling the components made by mission Indians and completing the new mission in two years. (Both, author's collection.)

Mission San Miguel, Arcángel attracted friendly natives, and several managed large properties that extended all the way to the coast, as well as inland. Several asistencias were established as outpost mission stations, including at Templeton, at Rancho de la Asunción to the south, at the Santa Lucia Mountains in 1816, and at Rancho del Playa. Fr. Juan Martinez made journeys into the interior to greet natives as far east as Lake Tulare, with an idea of developing more missions towards the foothills.

Reconstruction enabled reoccupation of the mission as a parish church by the Catholic Church in 1878. A long period followed during which Mission San Miguel, Arcángel was brought nearer to completion, including more modern efforts made in 1901 and 1928. In 2003, a severe earthquake caused structural damage to the adobe building, resulting in closure of portions for further renovation that continues into 2013. The mission, rededicated in 2009, is open to visitors with a church, chapel, and bookstore.

The skills necessary for efficient farming were learned easily by trustworthy mission Indians, allowing the missionaries to expand grazing and farming properties over 30,000 acres extending to the sea at San Simeon.

The missionaries introduced important trades, including blacksmithing, masonry, carpentry, soap making, weaving, and leather tooling, to the talented neophytes at all settlements. Cloisters off the portico housed padre quarters and segregated quarters for neophyte men and women. The mission Indians of neighboring Mission San Antonio and Mission San Luis Obispo had come to live and work at the new mission, also encouraging neophyte baptisms. The convert population grew to over 1,000 by 1814 and was comprised of Salinans and Yokuts.

The arcade of Mission San Miguel, Arcángel was begun in 1816 and completed by 1818. Its last resident priest, Fr. Ramon Abella, left in 1841. It was the last mission occupied by secular residents before being returned to the church in 1859.

At Mission San Miguel, Arcángel around 1934, the bell is mounted on a wooden scaffolding at the entry to the church to the left. The mission was thoroughly restored after 1928, proudly keeping its stone campanario (bell tower) restored outdoors.

Restorations of the mission would begin in earnest in 1901 and resume in 1921. In 2003, the San Simeon earthquake again closed Mission San Miguel, Arcángel for seismic reconstruction. After 2008, retrofitted walls left the delicate designs unharmed, and the mission has been made safe, although work will continue for many years to come. The mission church was rededicated in October 2009. (Southwest Museum of the American Indian Collection.)

In September 1897, the centennial of Mission San Miguel, Arcángel was celebrated with a three-day fiesta. At the side of the mission, 1,000 Indian neophytes rest; the mission's population reached its peak in 1814. (Southwest Museum of the American Indian Collection.)

Mission San Miguel, Arcángel became the last of the mission properties to be sold privately by Gov. Pío Pico on July 4, 1846, for an undisclosed amount. He transferred the title to William Reed and his family. Secular uses of the mission afterwards included offices, a hotel, a restaurant, a tavern, and sewing and shoe shops. The family living there met a tragic end from itinerant Gold Rush marauders. The return of the mission property to the Catholic Church occurred in 1859, and the church was reactivated in 1878, beginning an era of new authentic restorations at one of the most beautifully decorated of all 21 Alta California missions. Native art of similar quality and detail can be found only within Old Mission Santa Inés. Mission San Miguel, Arcángel, photographed in 1940, had been celebrated as one of the most successful and prosperous of the missions.

In 1928, Mission San Miguel, Arcángel was returned to the Franciscan Order, and at the monastery and parish church, restorations started in 1901 were largely completed. Mexican traditions, including Las Posadas, a Christmas re-enactment, were continued to modern times and held yearly at the mission.

Mission San Miguel, Arcángel survived through the years under caretakers such as Fr. Juan Cabot, who left in 1834 after 21 years in the face of the complete demise of the mission system. He accepted a grant from the governor to return to Spain.

By the end of the 19th century, mission Indians had given up tending herds, growing crops, and caring for orchards and vineyards.

The middle mission along El Camino Real, Mission San Miguel, Arcángel is situated directly at the center of old Alta California and directly in the path of El Camino Real. Traditionally, the trail roamed thousands of miles through Baja California, Central America, and Mexico and was taken by missionaries traveling through jungles or desert areas building the Spanish missions.

Intricate patterns were created after published drawings used by Estéban Munras. His skills were praised highly at Mission San Carlos Borromeo de Rio Carmelo, and he was known as a famed artisan trained to guide artistic neophytes to decorate wooden rails and wall frescos throughout the mission's plaster interior, as well as the ceiling and wooden beams of the church. Emigrants from Catalonia in Spain, Munras and Fr. Juan Martín, the head pastor, were friends and developed the work programs at Mission San Miguel, Arcángel during the 1820s.

The gallery at Mission San Miguel, Arcángel is cantilevered off the rear wall of the church, forming the choir loft. (Southwest Museum of the American Indian Collection.)

Mission San Miguel, Arcángel is pictured after the 1928 structural restorations were completed on the mission's church and surviving cloisters. Its archways were created asymmetrically with slightly unequal opening sizes, unlike other mission porticos. Neophyte Indians came into San Miguel to resettle from nearby Mission San Antonio and Mission San Luis Obispo. (Author's collection.)

Mission San Miguel, Arcángel's unique decorative wall paintings have the distinction of being the most authentically intact from artisan Estéban Munras, who in 1821 was hired to adorn the interior of the building, assisted by the mission Indians. The original artwork was meticulously restored with the glow of original hues. Many local types of seeds, clays, roots, and vegetable dyes, as well as minerals like cinnabar, natural tars, and other finds, created lasting warm colors.

A late-19th-century photograph shows a local in the courtyard of Mission San Miguel, Arcángel during its days as a parish church. (Southwest Museum of the American Indian Collection.)

Mission San Miguel, Arcángel was located within a fertile agricultural area and equipped with several agricultural tools, such as this olive press still surviving around 1880 after years of decaying weather. (Southwest Museum of the American Indian Collection.)

Mission San Miguel, Arcángel is documented here with a few remaining original buildings still standing within its extensive quadrangle forming the typical pueblo, a square connecting the orchards and vineyards.

Mission San Miguel, Arcángel's artwork was painted in 1821 in the 1816 church. The decorative walls create a background for the intricate wood railings and pulpit in this photograph. The pulpit, suspended from the wall with a crown soundboard and an octagonal base, displays a carving of the Madonna and Child at its far side. The crown panel suspends the image of a dove, representing the Holy Ghost, on the inner soundboard.

An asistencia, or sub-station of Mission San Miguel, Arcángel, is pictured in Templeton, California, in the early to mid-1900s. (Southwest Museum of the American Indian Collection.)

Ruins of the 1870s adobe asistencia of Mission San Miguel, Arcángel in Paso Robles, California, are seen in a photograph from the early to mid-1900s. (Southwest Museum of the American Indian Collection.)

Mission San Miguel, Arcángel was painted by California artist Oriana Weatherbee Day, who painted each mission in oils between 1877 and 1884, depicting daily life and the transitions of each mission's historical evolution.

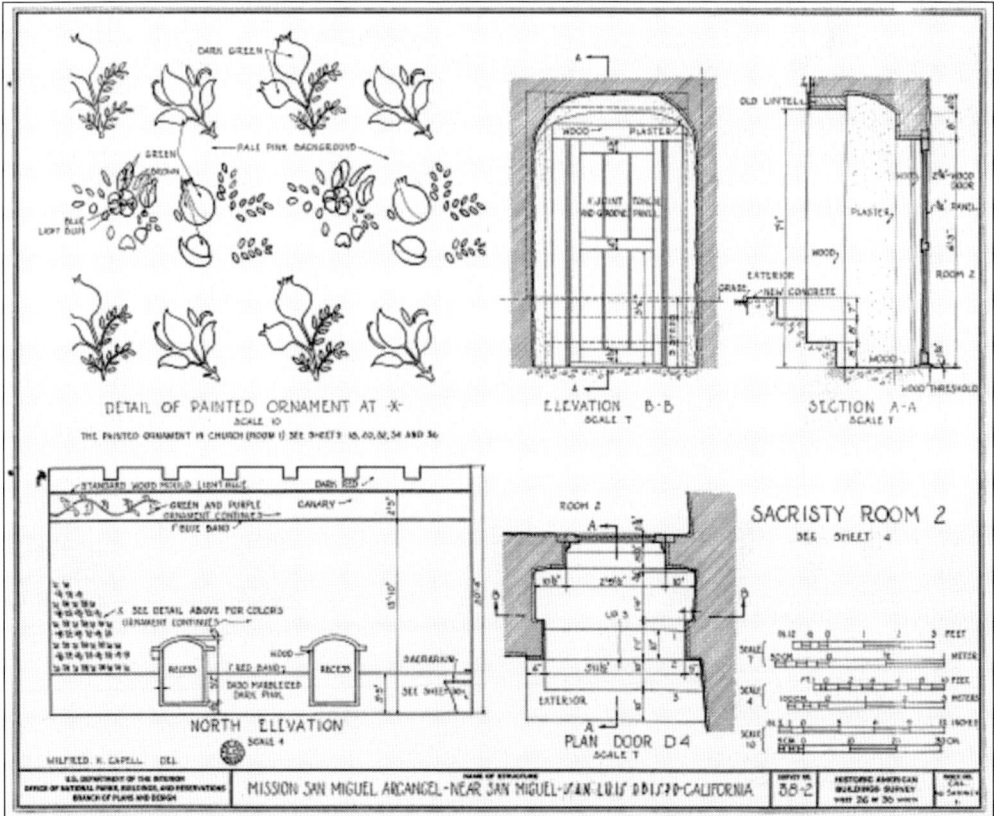

Estéban Munras, the talented painter from Monterey, had begun the interior of Mission San Miguel, Arcángel in 1835 and created with neophyte students an array of glowing floral patterns as decorative ornaments for walls, railings, ceilings, and beams. This mission is one of two, along with Mission Santa Inés, known for some of the best-restored original artwork of all mission interiors.

Mission San Miguel, Arcángel's irregular archways were studied and depicted in this elevation from the Library of Congress collection to guide the restorations beginning in 1928.

An elevation drawing depicts the irregular archways and clearly shows the present-day building in intricate detail. To complete accurate restorations of the mission, careful attention was paid both inside and out to details over 100 years old.

Six

HALLOWED GROUND
MISSION SANTA INÉS

The day of Mission Santa Inés's esteemed founding honored the feast of the Stigma of St. Francis, September 17, 1804. The 19th mission, it was named by Fr. Estévan Tápis, the recently chosen mission president. He was associated with the San Fernando College in Mexico City, and in its tradition first ritually blessed the water according to the rites of the Catholic Church. Then, he ceremonially blessed the mission and the buildings, dedicated to God and the Holy Ghost, erected a big cross, and sang the Litany of the Saints. This 1928 photograph shows the standing church. It was 139 feet long and 26 feet wide and was built in 1817 by Fr. Francisco Xavier Uría following the severe earthquake of 1812. (Anderson Family Collection.)

Pictured in a magic lantern slide from 1911, Mission Santa Inés suffered from a severe winter storm that collapsed its original bell tower. The old mission espadaña toppled, and it was later replaced by a less accurate framed shell emulating the original plastered design. A thoroughly accurate renovated espadaña was rebuilt to replace it by 1947. (Author's collection.)

The owner of this tourist photograph posed in front of Mission Santa Inés after 1915, about the date of this vintage "Tin Lizzie." California's Spanish missions became popular touring destinations for auto enthusiasts, and the development of El Camino Real included today's bells and road signs commemorating the first friars and their founding buildings. (Author's collection.)

Framed within the mission's graceful archway and posed at the garden's center, Fr. Vincent Kerwick continues the tradition of the mission gardens. Water was delivered from an elaborate system that began in the mountains several miles away. The early missionaries under Fr. Francisco Xavier Uría developed underground pipes and reservoirs that supplied the entire mission property. Conduits fed water to adobes, including an old Indian village nearby. (Anderson Family Collection.)

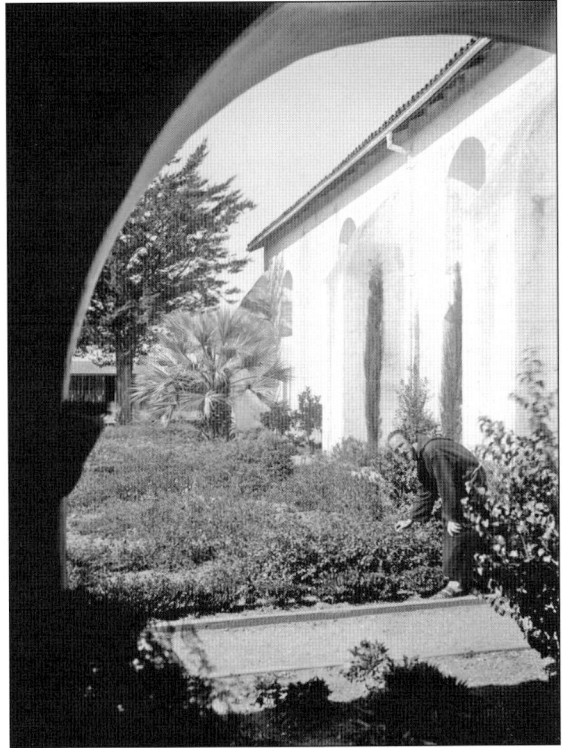

The mission of 1817 was rebuilt with thick adobe walls and roofed with clay tiles. The south wall was veneered with *ladrillos* (burned brick or protective tile) to resist the wet southern storms of California, greatly affecting the old adobe's strength. (Author's collection.)

Mission Santa Inés, photographed around 1900, shows the existing church from 1817, complete with adobe walls nearly five feet thick. The belfry is original. In 1833, Zacatecan Franciscans arrived, prior to the impending secularization period at the settlement. In 1824, changing mission life had led to soldiers being attacked by discontented neophytes. Many buildings, including the mission, were burned to the ground. A new padre, Fr. Blas Ordaz, began to restore the grounds, rebuilding damaged sections. In 1917, a rededication of the church followed the efforts of Fr. Alexander Buckler's restorations, and he retired in 1924. Capuchin Franciscans, within the order since the 16th century, were brought to oversee the mission, and today remain as the caretakers.

The mission is pictured in 1928 after its modern restorations. By 1842, the new bishop, Garcia Diego, was installed at Mission Santa Bárbara to oversee both Baja and Alta California. He restored 36,000 acres known as College Rancho that were historically part of Mission Santa Inés after initiating an ecclesiastical school and the first educational institution in California. (Anderson Family Collection.)

In 1882, noticeable improvements were made to the Mission Santa Inés buildings while a stonemason and builder lived there. From 1904 through 1930, Father Buckler carried out an intensive program of preservation. The Capuchin Franciscan friar Fr. Vincent Kerwick was placed in charge of the mission and became head pastor, keeping a long lineage into modern times of overseeing the mission history. (Anderson Family Collection.)

The original tower of adobe and brick fell during a storm in 1911 and was rebuilt from reinforced concrete. Outlines of the original tower were followed somewhat in the new structure, but three archways were used in the lower tier, out of character with the original, and the walls were made much thinner. It was rebuilt and restored by 1947. (Anderson Family Collection.)

Twenty-seven neophytes were baptized at the mission on its founding day in 1804. Thousands of indigenous people lived nearby in the foothills, and many were more than content to live their pastoral lifestyle within tribal communities. Only 1,411 became baptized over the next 32 years, and the mission's greatest population of 768 was reached in 1816.

Fr. Francisco Xavier Uría laid the foundation stones for the church standing today and dedicated it in 1817. In this photograph of Mission Santa Inés from 1928, a resident friar, Fr. Vincent Kerwick, poses contentedly in front of the ancient monastery cloister. (Anderson Family Collection.)

Father Kerwick, pastor of Mission Santa Inés in 1932, carries on a tradition of service at the mission under the order of the Capuchin Franciscans. The friars honored their tradition of living within the catacomb chapels and burial crypts lined with their bones under a plaque with the inscription: "What you are now, we used to be. What we are now, you will be." (Anderson Family Collection.)

At Mission Santa Inés, the altar's wooden statue features Saint Agnes centered in a niche said to be carved by one or more of the mission Indians in honor of the church's namesake. The mission's rich collection of restored artifacts includes handmade vestments, early handmade parchment music books, and Latin missals. It has one of the largest collections of Alta California mission artwork within the state, including the 14 Stations of the Cross, painted in 1642.

Our Lady of the Rosary is a sculpture with stunning detail from the Mexican Baroque period of the mid-18th century that was preserved at the beginning of the 20th century through the work of Mamie Goulet, niece of Fr. Alexander Buckler. Mission Santa Inés has the largest and most valuable collection of early California church vestments, some predating many California missions themselves. Besides a repository for sacred art and liturgical items from abandoned Mission La Purísima Concepción nearby, the mission's collection of early vestments came from original Mexican and Lower Baja missions. Father Junípero Serra's journals in 1769 noted preserving the relics while in Baja California. The collection contains a vestment worn by Father Serra during the period of Alta California's settlement.

The richly painted reredos contains individual niches that hold the most honored saints and include a four-foot native carving of the namesake of Mission Santa Inés Virgen y Mártir, Saint Agnes, in the highest place above the altar. Native paintings glow with marbleized green hues after restoration that carefully removed many previous coatings.

The Old Mission Santa Inés choir loft, perched above the eastern entry, was flooded by brilliant sunlight pouring through the nave forward to the altar during sunrise services.

After 1812, reconstruction of the damaged buildings began with a new and much larger church built of adobe and brick. Facing east, it measured nearly 140 feet long, 25 feet wide, and 30 feet high with heavily buttressed walls five feet thick. Pine timbers were brought from the San Rafael Mountains as supports for the clay-tile roofing. A new belfry had been constructed, and the church was dedicated on July 4, 1817.

An 1875 photograph shows the barren surroundings of Old Mission Santa Inés. In 1833, the Franciscan College of Guadalupe at Zacatecas, Mexico, sent fathers to minister to mission populations during the period of Mexico's independence. The head missionaries were charged to eventually give up control to secular administrator José Ramirez, and in an 1836 inventory, he valued the mission at $50,000. The mission was sold in 1846 by Gov. Pío Pico for $7,000 but returned to the church after 1862, just 12 years past California's admission to statehood. (Southwest Museum of the American Indian Collection.)

The coastal native home of the Island Chumash was near Santa Barbara, and their populations spread east to the Santa Ynez Mountains and to Mission Santa Inés. The Chumash developed an astronomical system that compares favorably to European systems in terms of accuracy. Their economy was based on their abilities as artisans, ranchers, and fishermen, and colonies consisted of large huts built from poles with tule reeds along the coastline. Nearly 20,000 gathered and leached acorns and harvested nuts, seeds, and berries. The Chumash also hunted animals, although their only tools were made from flint. They were skilled at constructing sea-going plank canoes often holding a dozen or more, sealed tightly by asphalt material and capable of navigating the coastal waters.

The historic 19th archway, still standing today, is one of 24 original archways at Old Mission Santa Inés. Before 1823, the mission had established a gristmill for corn and wheat and a unique fulling mill to cleanse wool and soften cloth, later woven by industries spread throughout the settlement. Cattle were used to create tallow and hides in order to generate funds. In later years, mission fathers were constantly needing to pay Chumash labor and to feed and cloth soldiers, as secular laws exacted taxes on each mission under Mexico's government.

A close-up view shows one of Mission Santa Inés's bells. It was designed to swing with less effort, using a balance weight at the top to help ring it. Three original bells were cast and obtained by the mission friars in 1807, 1817, and 1818. After a storm collapsed the tower in 1911, a cast concrete tower was erected resembling the original but adding a fourth window opening. The cast concrete espadaña, considered out of character with the original, was replaced with another that resembled the first tower more accurately. The new tower was completed in 1947 using three windows exactly like the original campanario of 1817. (Southwest Museum of the American Indian Collection.)

This confessional from the mid-19th century had carvings added by Chumash, among many early decorations and relics existing today within the church. Old Mission Santa Inés is considered well preserved and authentically restored after considerable modern archeology to curate the site. (Southwest Museum of the American Indian Collection.)

One of two main reservoirs of burned brick created by Father Uría to furnish water throughout the mission complex is pictured here. This one measures 60 feet long and was filled by a series of connected underground pipes and flumes to move water from mountain streams. (Southwest Museum of the American Indian Collection.)

With Mission Santa Inés in view, the tannery overseen by mission Indians is among many ruins of what were once developed, diversified industries in the settlement. Most adobe buildings were reduced to earthen mounds and declined rapidly during secularization. The mission grazed up to 13,000 cattle at the height of its prosperity.

An All Souls' Day graveside ceremony, pictured at the beginning of the 20th century, continues the tradition from the founding days. The four bells in this tower were later changed back to three when the espadaña that crumbled during the storm of 1911 was replaced. (Southwest Museum of the American Indian Collection.)

Foundations of the tannery that had been owned and operated by the mission are shown in this photograph from the American Historic Building Survey. Water was fed into a reservoir, channeled through a gateway, and spilled into masonry basins to begin the process of curing leather hides.

Viewed here from the southeast, the mission had been continuously worked on over the years. Fr. Alexander Buckler took charge in 1904, and during the next 20 years, he was devoted to restoring many buildings and broken equipment. After his death, the mission served to house a line of Capuchin Franciscan padres lasting to modern times.

This portrait at Mission San Luis Obispo de Tolosa shows Saint Agnes, also known as Santa Ynez or Santa Inés, the namesake of Mission Santa Inés. Fr. Alexander Buckler's early attention to restorations at Mission Santa Inés began in 1904. After the storm of 1911 crumbled the original espadaña and three buttresses of the church's exterior walls, a new, earnest effort to preserve the mission began. The Hearst Foundation provided further funding into 1962, at which time the mission was led by Fr. Timothy O'Sullivan. (Southwest Museum of the American Indian Collection.)

Populated territories surrounding Mission Santa Inés were of keen interest to the padres. Gov. José Joaquín de Arrillaga sent 10 soldiers with the founding party over the dirt trail leading to the high foothills of the Santa Ynez River Valley. Fr. Estévan Tápis blessed the site, founding the mission on September 17, 1804.

After reconstruction from the disastrous storm of 1911 that toppled three buttresses of the church walls at the northwest corner, near the cemetery at the base of its giant footing, photographs and measurements were taken of Mission Santa Inés, along with all the other missions, for the Historic American Building Survey, preserved by the Library of Congress.

This view of Mission Santa Inés shows the rear of the church building at the left. During the prosperity of the 1820s, the structures were built around an open quadrangle. They included the church, padres' house, workshops, storerooms, tannery, blacksmith shop, and industry buildings.

The mission's bells play an important role, signaling the hour of prayers and services from the nearly 40-foot-tall espadaña. Traditionally, this began with the first friars harnessing their cherished bells along strong limbs of live oak trees, several ringing at once to beckon native neophytes into the church.

Mission Santa Inés was an important part of California's channel mission chain. It was founded in 1804 by Fr. Estévan Tápis and served as a connection between San Diego and Santa Barbara to the south and points north on El Camino Real. This photograph was produced by the American Historic Building Survey.

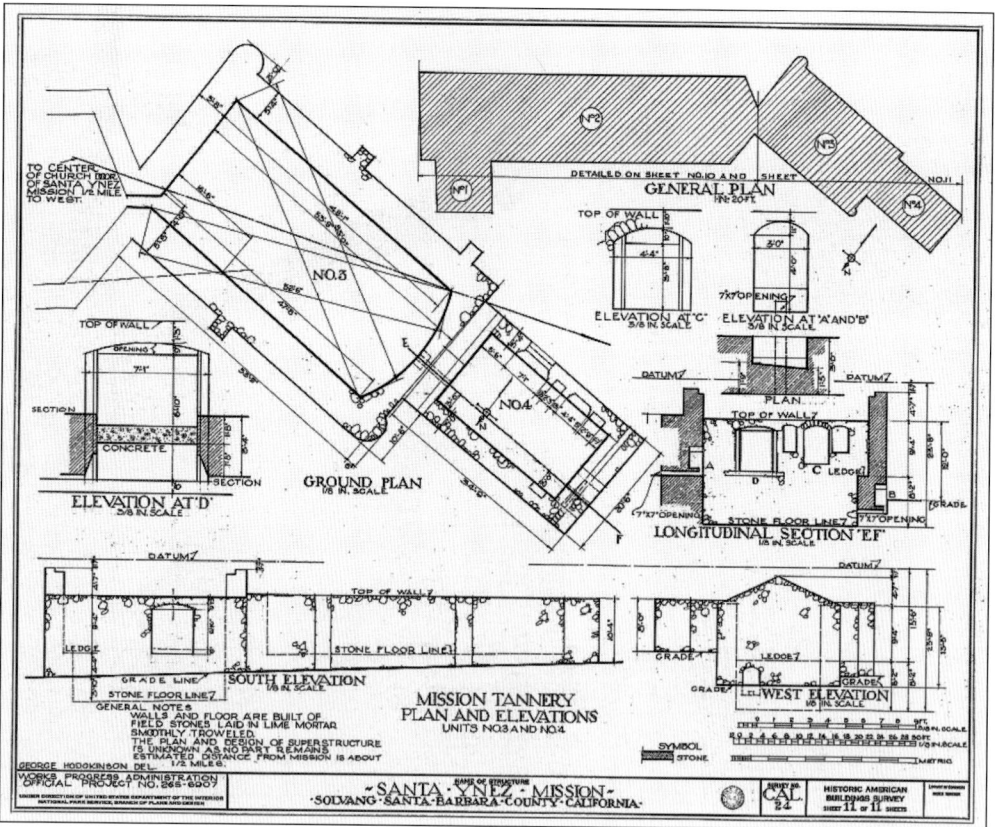

All missions were rebuilt according to carefully prepared plans that reveal interesting features of California's oldest buildings. Earthquakes and weather damage had created the most problems for buildings made of adobe and brick and mortar. Many artisans were required to perform intricate and specialized tasks to bring the buildings back to life.

Seven

CALIFORNIA'S MISSIONS PAST AND PRESENT
TOURING EL CAMINO REAL

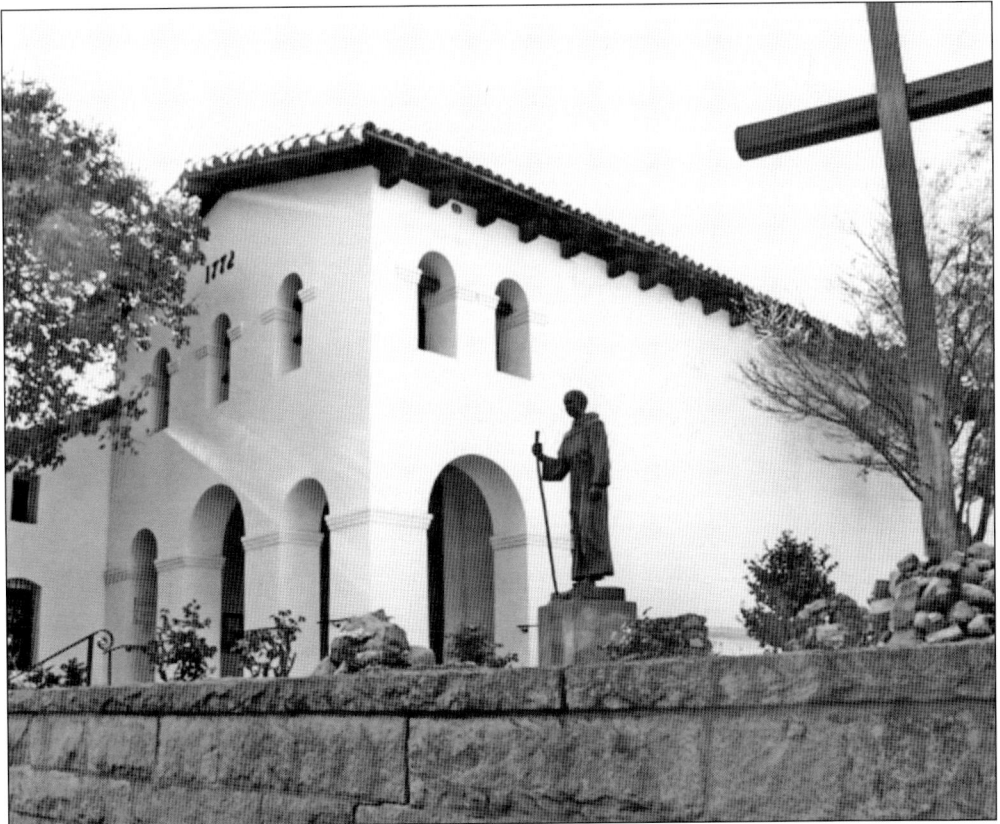

Mission San Luis Obispo de Tolosa has stood since Father Serra first blessed the spot on the day of its founding, September 1, 1772. The monastery to the left of the church had a portico built in 1794, and it was walled in by 1894, then restored in 1933. Today, the mission can be visited at Old Mission Parish, 751 Palm Street in San Luis Obispo or online at www.missionsanluisobispo.org. Phone the parish at 805-781-8220. (Author's collection.)

Mission San Luis Obispo de Tolosa is set in the middle of San Luis Obispo, a colorful town and agricultural area known for high-quality California wines and produce. The fully restored mission is an easy walk while visiting downtown. The windows of its espadaña reveal the authentic bells that were brought by the friars to the mission. (Both, author's collection.)

The first of the "Channel Missions" had been planned years ahead of its founding by Mexico City's visitor-general of Spain and was an early vision of Father Serra's to establish a settlement midway on the Alta California coast between Mission San Carlos Borromeo and Mission San Diego de Alcalá. He founded Mission San Buenaventura on March 31, 1782, honoring the popular Italian Saint Bonaventure. The mission is located at 211 East Main Street in Ventura. Phone 805-643-4318 or visit www.sanbuenaventuramission.org (Author's collection.)

The unique beauty of Mission San Buenaventura's compound and courtyard, gardens, and patio makes the mission a perfect stop for many locals as well as tourists seeking to capture the authentic flavor of the original California Spanish missions. (Author's collection.)

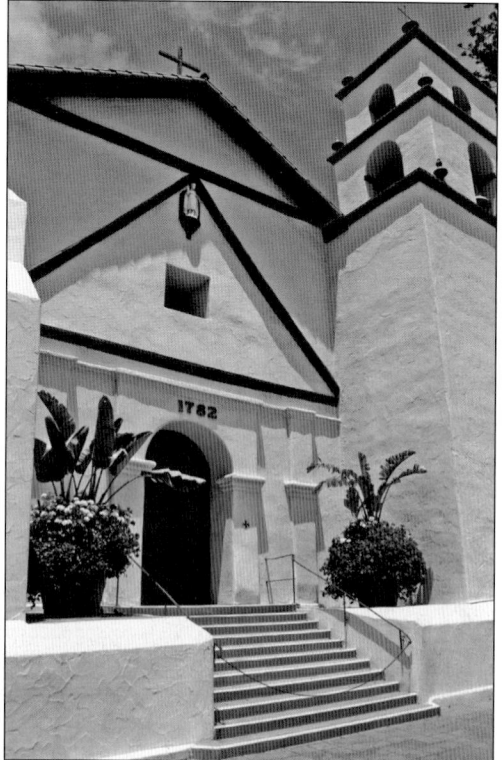

Mission San Buenaventura was the last to be founded by Father Serra on March 1, 1782. Reconstructed after a major earthquake in 1812, the mission was completed in 1816, at a time when Fr. Francisco Palóu estimated native Coastal Chumash to number nearly 20,000 spread out in several settlements. (Author's collection.)

The Spanish-Moorish-style fountain at Mission Santa Bárbara, Virgen y Mártir was built in 1808. Water ran over to the lavanderia, where Indian women knelt to clean clothing in a stone laundry basin. The mission is located at 2201 Laguna Street in Santa Barbara. Phone 805-682-4713 or 805-682-4149 for the gift shop. Visit www.santabarbaramission.org for more information. (Author's collection.)

Mission Santa Bárbara's church and monastery are a large complex of buildings that have been overseen from their founding by the Franciscan fathers. (Author's collection.)

The arcade of Mission Santa Bárbara's monastery is set in lush gardens that date back to the early settlement and display common species collected over the centuries from visitors. (Author's collection.)

At Mission Santa Bárbara's entry, a statue of Father Serra greets visitors to the mission. The year 2013 marks the 300th anniversary of the birth of Father Serra, the legendary founder of the mission system of Alta California that began in San Diego in 1769. His home was Majorca, an island near Spain. (Author's collection.)

Mission San Miguel, Arcángel, founded in 1797 by Fr. Fermín de Francisco Lasuén, is 16th in the lineage in California. The mission is located at 775 Mission Street in San Miguel. Phone 805-467-3256 for the gift shop, and the Web site is www.missionsanmiguel.org. (Author's collection.)

Mission San Miguel, Arcángel's 2,000-pound bell (center) sits in the campanario behind the mission building. It is an impressively built stone tower with an unusual design unlike any other California mission. (Author's collection.)

The surrounding quadrangle of Mission San Miguel, Arcángel has many interesting features distinguishing it. The standing church was completed in 1818 and was rededicated after extensive repairs following the San Simeon earthquake, some of which are still being carried out in several phases. The completed work includes a gift shop and museum (6,010 square feet), convento and museum (10,973 square feet), retreat wing (6,205 square feet), and tailor shop and refectory (5,849 square feet). Projects yet to be completed are the friars' residence and retreat rooms (7,205 square feet), friars' library and chapel (5,849 square feet), and church, sacristy, and cemetery (34,996 square feet). (Author's collection.)

Mission La Purísima Concepción de María de Santísima is a historical example of an extensive system of mission buildings in California. From this mission south, El Camino Real continues near the edge of the sea and connects the four missions of the Santa Barbara Channel. Visit this beautiful California State Historic Park at 2295 Purisima Road in Lompoc. Phone 805-733-3713 or visit www.lapurisimamission.org. (Both, author's collection.)

Old Mission Santa Inés is located in the fertile agricultural Santa Ynez Valley, an area renowned for its wines. About 30 miles from Santa Barbara, it is located at 1760 Mission Drive in Solvang. Phone 805-688-4815 or visit www.missionsantaines.org. The mission is an active parish church. (Author's collection.)

Immersed in the pioneer history of California, Old Mission Santa Inés is known for its fine collection of early vestments and liturgical artifacts and stands as a monument to the traditions of the earliest settlers in California. (Author's collection.)

Mission Santa Inés is dedicated to Saint Agnes of Rome. A revered martyr, she was sentenced to death for refusing betrothal of marriage and accepted the punishment. Her sainthood is symbolized by the lamb of sacrifice, the emblem of the faithful. Old Mission Santa Inés, Virgin y Mártyr was 19th in the chain of 21 missions created over the lifetime of Spain's conquest. Mission San Francisco Solano, founded on July 14, 1823, would be the last Franciscan stronghold, falling immediately under secular rule. Gen. Mariano Vallejo staked out his last stand for Mexico, surrendering obligingly after a minor skirmish in which mission residents confronted US general John C. Frémont and his small band of cavalry during the Bear Flag Rebellion of 1846. (Author's collection.)

Within walking distance from Old Mission Santa Inés remain the adobe buildings that were part of the industries at the settlement. An area of adobe buildings nearby also housed neophytes who worked at the mission. (Author's collection.)

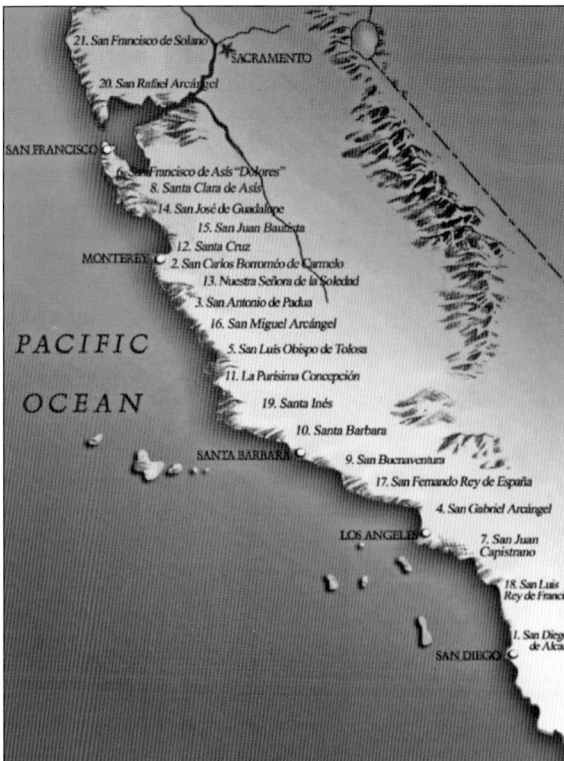

El Camino Real is the path reaching all the Spanish missions, and many are separated by about a day's journey, forming a chain. The earliest trails between jungle missions extended from Guatemala and Mexico over thousands of miles and were developed by missionaries coming to Baja and Alta California. Father Serra dreamed of mission colonies throughout Alta California, and Franciscan settlements grew to 21 main missions and several asistencias and smaller estancia stations.